CHOOSE

YOUR BLUEPRINT TO
FINANCIAL INDEPENDENCE

CHRIS MAMULA + BRAD BARRETT
+ JONATHAN MENDONSA

ISBN: 978-0-9600589-0-7 (Paperback)

ISBN: 978-0-9600589-1-4 (Hardcover)

Library of Congress Control Number: 2018965588

All content reflects our opinion at a given time and can change as time progresses. All information should be taken as three guy's opinions and should not be misconstrued for professional or legal advice.

Front cover image and Book Design by Ellie Schroeder

Printed by Choose FI Media, Inc., in the United States of America.

First printing edition 2019.

Choose FI Media, Inc.
P.O. Box 3982
Glen Allen, VA, 23058

www.choosefi.com

chooseFI

DEDICATION

We dedicate this book to our children
Anna and Molly Barrett, Brynn Mamula
and Zachary and Rees Mendonsa.
You are our daily reminders of what is
important in life and our inspiration to
try to make the world a better place.

CONTENTS

EARN MORE

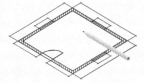

INVEST BETTER

WHAT'S NEXT

NOTE TO READERS

This book takes the cumulative knowledge of the financial independence (FI) community and distills it into principles that you can use to build a FI lifestyle quickly. Many members of the FI community share their stories on the ChooseFI podcast, and those interviews are the basis of this book.

Many of those featured produce content on their own blogs, podcasts, in books, or through other mediums. If we used ideas or quotes not directly shared on the podcast, they are attributed in the text and cited in the bibliography.

For clarity and ease of reading, not all quotes are attributed in the text of the book. If a quote is not clearly attributed, it was collected from ChooseFI podcast interview archives. ChooseFI podcast episodes referenced in each chapter are indexed in the back of the book for those interested in learning more about an individual's story, diving more deeply into their content, or hearing the full context of a conversation.

Many people interviewed on the Choose FI podcast choose to share their stories anonymously. To respect their privacy and for consistency throughout the book, we refer to people as they were referred to on the podcast unless they specifically requested otherwise or have revealed their full identity in other public forums.

PART 1

GETTING STARTED

The story
you tell yourself
becomes
your reality.

CHAD KELLOGG
AMERICAN ALPINIST

INTRODUCTION

BY: CHRIS MAMULA

CREATE
YOUR OWN
FI STORY

accomplished my goal of financial independence (FI) and retired at forty-one years of age, sixteen and a half years after beginning my career as a physical therapist. Friday, December 1, 2017, was my last day at my job.

So how did I spend the first Monday of the rest of my life, a day when I could do whatever I want? You're reading it.

I started the day with my usual morning routine of reading and quiet time, a workout, and breakfast with my wife and daughter. It was much like any other Monday, only without all the rushing of having somewhere to be. I dropped my daughter off at preschool, then took a nice long walk through the park next to my house to clear my head and breathe in the crisp late fall air. By nine thirty a.m., I sat down at my computer to begin the book you're now reading.

Did I always have a passion for writing? No. Was writing a book, *another* personal finance book at that, my life's dream? No! But it is the thing that I most want to be doing with my life right now.

This is the book that I have been seeking for the past fifteen years and have not been able to find. I didn't decide I wanted to write this book. I became convinced that I *needed* to. This is the book that could have saved me six, if not seven, figures in financial mistakes and years of angst and unhappiness that I experienced on the path to FI because I was pursuing the wrong things. I am confident it will change your life.

FI is not about retiring early or retiring at all really. It's all about having the freedom and flexibility to design *your* life in alignment with *your* values. You can work on things important to you. You can work at your own pace. Or you can choose not to work at all. FI gives you the power to decide. It allows you to use your money as a tool to live a rich life, freeing yourself from the need to go to a job.

Building wealth that enables FI is simple, but it's not easy. There is a diverse group of people featured in this book who have taken different paths to FI, but we each have only the same three tools to use in pursuit of our FI goals:

1. Spend Less
2. Earn More
3. Invest Better

Each tool serves as a theme for a section of the book.

However, the growing financial independence community is about much more than becoming wealthy, retiring early, or any other financial theme. We align our money with our values to build the lives we want rather than the ones we're "supposed" to live. This requires intentionality, doing things differently than the majority who surround you.

Those of you who choose to follow through on the lessons in this book will find that FI is not only a possibility but a mathematical certainty. Equally important, you can get there faster than you could have imagined! Instead of staying in careers until the traditional age of sixty-five or seventy, the principles in this book can make work optional for those in their early sixties, fifties, forties, thirties, or for a rare few, in their twenties.

Finding purpose is vital to getting started down the path to FI. I'm hopeful that FI will enable and inspire people to use their freedom to pursue opportunities to make the world a better place. For you, this may mean trying to change the world, your local community, or your own family. It may simply mean becoming a better version of yourself. It may mean retirement in the traditional sense of leaving paid work and living on your investments. Or it may mean using your financial freedom to pursue a new career or start a business you would otherwise be afraid to try.

Finding purpose and living intentionally are key components to achieving FI and designing the life you truly want. This book helps you get started by finding your personal "why" and then giving you the tools to design a life consistent with *your* values.

YOU GET TO CHOOSE

This book is called *Choose FI*. It would be easy to focus on FI, financial independence, and classify this as a personal finance book. But don't overlook the word *choose*. This is a book about making choices.

There are two paths that you can take through life. You can follow the standard path, or you can *Choose FI*. This initial decision is followed by many subsequent decisions, allowing you to build the life you desire. This book was designed to be a guide to assist you on that journey, a choose-your-own-adventure book if you will. You can pick and choose the levers you want to pull as you design your personalized path to FI.

I started life heading down the standard path. I was conditioned from a young age to get "good grades" so I could go to a "good college." Getting a degree would enable me to get a "good" (i.e., a high paying) job. This would allow me to live the American dream of owning a nice house in a good neighborhood, taking two to four weeks of vacation each year, and retiring at age sixty-five.

Shortly after starting my job as a physical therapist, I realized the career I had chosen, and the standard American professional lifestyle that accompanied it were not, in fact, what I wanted after all. Like many people, I felt trapped.

I spent seven years of my life and tens of thousands of dollars on degrees that enabled me to get what was supposed to be my "dream job." My wife and I then bought our "dream house." Unfortunately, we soon realized we were living someone else's dream.

I got the idea that early retirement was the solution to my problems, though I had no idea if it was possible or how to do it. I randomly chose the goal to retire by age forty. I started to educate myself on the technical aspects of personal finance like investing, tax strategies, and retirement planning. Despite being diligent savers, I learned standard advice was keeping us stuck on the standard path rather than enabling financial independence. The financial advice we received was conflicted, deceptive, and unnecessarily expensive.

It's easy to find yourself on the standard path. Most people in our society live paycheck to paycheck. Many people are paying for past decisions like taking out student loans, which were often made before they were old enough to buy alcohol legally. Homes serve as status symbols. Time and money are spent to keep them up by homeowners who rarely have time to enjoy them. Financed cars depreciate while being used primarily to transport people to and from work. Any extra money is spent on "retail therapy," restaurant meals, and happy hours that people "deserve" because they work so damned hard to keep the hamster wheel spinning.

Paying to maintain this lifestyle leaves little financial margin. Things go wrong from time to time. Living paycheck to paycheck comes with the privilege of getting to pay interest to a credit card company—at an average annual percentage rate of 16 percent—which you need to help you stay afloat.

It's hard to know how many people choose this lifestyle consciously, but regardless, it is the norm for most Americans. Most gradually slide further into a hole that keeps them trapped on this standard path.

Similarly, most people say relationships and family are the most important things in their lives, but a job is where they spend the majority of their time and energy. Why do people stay in lifestyles so out of alignment with their stated values?

Those who want something better and are good savers go to financial advisors because we've heard how complicated investing is. We pay excessive fees and taxes following the usual advice that keeps us trapped on the standard path. Most advisors receive commissions for the sale of financial products or are paid as a percentage of the assets you have invested with them. This incentivizes the financial industry to unnecessarily complicate investing, so clients remain dependent on them. It's also in their best interest for clients to always strive for more rather than determine how much is "enough."

What dreams do people give up on because they drift down the standard path through life? How many people don't start their business because they're afraid they will fail? How many people don't take that trip of a lifetime because they can't afford it or can't get vacation time approved? How many marriages start filled with hope, promise, and romance only to crumble under the strain of financial stress and time demands that burden so many?

When you *Choose FI*, you are choosing a way of life with more options and less fear. You're choosing to live life in alignment with your values. FI provides freedom. It's easy to see why *Choosing FI* is appealing. So why do so few people do it? Why do so many fail to diverge from the standard path despite its limitations? One reason is simply the fact that the standard path is . . . the standard. It's the norm. The standard path is deeply ingrained by schools, families, media, and popular culture. Above all else, most people have never thought that there might be a different way. We all know people on the standard path. We have all probably been on that path as well. It's a challenge to take a different path without anyone to guide you.

Author and motivational speaker Jim Rohn frequently said,

"You are the average of the five people you spend the most time with."

The examples in this book and the people you'll meet in the FI community will provide a new normal to which you can recalibrate your life.

As you learn the stories of people who *Choose FI*, you'll quickly see the standard path has many exits that most people bypass because they don't realize they exist. *Choosing FI* doesn't require extreme frugality, a massive income, or special investing prowess. It starts with questioning the things that trap so many of us on the standard path and understanding that there is a different way.

FINDING MY PATH

I began learning about personal finance by reading books and articles on my own, with no particular method to navigate all of the available information. I listened to radio show hosts like Dave Ramsey, targeted to an audience working themselves out of debt I no longer had, because that was the most readily available information, and I could listen when driving in my car.

Reading and listening gave me a basic foundation in mainstream personal finance. But my wife and I were already avoiding debt. We bought a house we could afford and were paying it off quickly. We were saving roughly 50 percent of our income, far exceeding the traditionally recommended 10 to 15 percent.

On a particularly bad day at work, I typed the words "extreme early retirement" into the search box on my computer screen. Up popped what would become the first blog I ever read, Early Retirement Extreme (ERE). My life was changed forever!

I dove headfirst into the world of Jacob Lund Fisker at ERE and took on the journey through his "21 Day Makeover" to early retirement. It included ways to get our expenses as low as possible to be able to retire as soon as possible. On day three, Fisker's program suggested I could "learn to cook based on a small set of staples (rice, beans, onions). These staples are then bought in 10 lbs bags." I guess my love of sushi and microbrews would have to go.

On day seven, Fisker suggested "going car free." On subsequent days, he advised getting rid of the cell phone, cable TV, and most of the other things that I associated with a normal life. He shared how he was able to live on under $10,000 per year. It seemed like a lot of sacrifices, but it might just be worth it. I wanted out of the standard American lifestyle, and I wanted out bad. I thought I found my ticket.

I found my tribe among Financial Independence, Retire Early (FIRE) bloggers. They showed me that the life I dreamed of could become my reality. Reading these blogs was highly motivational and educational. Unfortunately, reading them also had unintended consequences. Three things happened that made me far less happy.

First, as my knowledge of investing and tax planning grew, I couldn't help but continue to glance in the rearview mirror, where I would see all the past blunders we made when we'd followed conventional wisdom and mainstream advice. Our investing mistakes were particularly painful because we paid an advisor handsomely for awful guidance. I spent a lot of time looking back with regret and bitterness.

Second, FIRE blogs put early retirement on a pedestal, so in my mind, early retirement became a nirvana. I felt the need to retire early. *Then* I could be happy. I stopped appreciating all the amazing things that I already had in my life. I lost the ability to be the carefree, happy-go-lucky person I used to be. Between glancing back at our past mistakes and looking forward to early retirement, I found myself unable to enjoy the present.

Third, while gaining a deeper understanding of our finances was initially a positive thing, I became overly focused on money. I focused on getting our expenses as low as possible so I could retire as soon as possible. I began to scrutinize every dollar that left our household. Before the FIRE blogs, my wife and I gave freely to charities and other causes we believed in. Now I acted judgmentally. Was this organization as effective and efficient as we were with our money? Would that person use our gift wisely or just waste it? How could we justify giving away our hard-earned money when saving it would allow us to retire sooner? We took similar approaches with our personal spending, tightly holding on to every dollar. We began to do less of the things that had always made us happy.

Rather than gaining the freedom I desired, I led myself into a different trap. I was trying to live up to what I believed to be other people's values and expectations rather than being true to my own.

Hitting these potholes is common for many of us who *Choose FI*. I finally realized that I needed to figure out what I truly wanted in life. I needed to develop my own personal blueprint for building that life. I needed to learn that money is a very powerful tool that can provide many things, but it is always just a means to an end and never the end itself. This sent me on a mission of discovery, looking for truth.

I began questioning everything and reading voraciously, from technical aspects of personal finance to finding personal happiness, fulfillment, and purpose. I accumulated different lessons and truths from a wide variety of sources that applied to my own life and kept them. At the same time, I took the parts that didn't fit what I wanted for my life and threw them away. Gradually, a personalized plan began to emerge that worked for my family and me.

As this happened, I felt myself becoming a happier and more empowered person. I began to see the positive effects again that financial independence could have, enabling me to pursue a variety of fulfilling paths at different stages in life.

I began to think about how to help others, each on their own individual journeys to FI. Each of you has personal strengths, weaknesses, past experiences, needs, and preferences. How could I help you reach financial independence quickly, empowering you to do whatever you desire with your life? How could I help you avoid the massive mistakes that I had made wasting a decade on a suboptimal financial path? How could I help you avoid driving yourself to the brink of depression by trying to live up to the standards of gurus whose philosophies, circumstances, strengths, and weaknesses did not match up exactly to your own?

While mimicking any single philosophy contributed to making financial and personal mistakes, I found truths in each of them. What if I started a podcast? I could interview a group of people who had overcome their own challenges and found their own truths while achieving FI quickly. I could take these lessons and look at common themes and patterns to develop principles that anyone could use to develop their own personalized path to achieve this rare yet very achievable outcome of financial independence.

A few months after this idea began rattling around in my head, I stumbled upon a new podcast, *Choose FI*. I listened to a few episodes. One of the hosts, Brad Barrett, was at a stage in life similar to my own. Co-host Jonathan Mendonsa was at a point where I had been a few years earlier. He had a palpable excitement to go down this road and a desire to grow and learn, but with some obvious blind spots that I was able to spot quickly due to my own past mistakes.

I found myself rooting for them to be bad and fail. I viewed them as competitors who beat me to the punch in doing exactly what I wanted to do with the podcast. However, as I listened to them, I couldn't help but to become a huge fan and see that these guys got it and were building something special.

It made no sense to try to reinvent the wheel and compete with them. Instead, I contacted them and asked if they would be interested in teaming up. I would use their interviews as the basis for this book, which could be another outlet for the life-changing message of FI. They agreed, and we proceeded full speed ahead.

This book exists because we feel FI is a superpower that can radically transform your life, relationships, financial stability, and ultimately your happiness. There's normally so much stress surrounding money, but when you can reframe saving money to helping you pursue what you truly want out of life, it becomes the obvious choice.

I'm Brad Barrett, a suburban husband and father of two young daughters, former CPA who left my corporate job at thirty-five to pursue entrepreneurship and shortly after declared my Financial Independence. Jonathan Mendonsa and I started the ChooseFI podcast in 2017, and the message has resonated with people all across the world. In partnership with Chris Mamula, this book represents the best of our podcast and the FI message.

BRAD

In the summer of 2016, I heard Brad as a guest on the Mad Fientist podcast talking about credit card travel rewards. When I found out he lived in Richmond, VA, I reached out to see if he wanted to get lunch. My enthusiasm got the best of me and a fun conversation on pursuing FI and maximizing travel rewards morphed into an idea to start and collaborate on a blog and companion podcast. The concepts brought together by this community are powerful enough to start a movement. While it's difficult to have a blog or podcast be linear, especially when you are learning as you go, this book represents our best effort to distill those transformative ideas into a Blueprint to FI.

JONATHAN

This book features stories of people who have achieved or are on the path to FI. On the podcast, Brad often says FI is like a superpower that makes life easier. However, there are no Clark Kents or Peter Parkers in this book. No one in this book is from the planet Krypton, and no one was bitten by a radioactive spider.

This book is filled with stories of ordinary people from all walks of life. You will read about people from rural areas with low costs of living and high-cost big cities, from an assortment of careers ranging from physicians and hedge fund managers to school teachers and military service members, from ultra-creative entrepreneurs to those who have worked only regular nine-to-five jobs. You'll hear from those who embrace frugality as a virtue to those who travel the world uninhibited. This book features those whose investment choices range from stocks and bonds to real estate to their own businesses and any combination of the above.

While there are differences among the people featured in this book, they share three common threads. Each person:

- **Challenges limiting beliefs and looks at the world in a non-standard way.**

- **Takes definitive actions to improve their life.**

- **Finds a way to utilize their own unique strengths and values and chooses to define success on their own terms.**

Everyone you will get to know in this book has created their own superpowers. Through the principles they embrace, you can develop your own as well.

Every revolutionary idea seems to evoke
three stages of reaction. They may be
summed up by the phrases:

1. It's completely impossible.
2. It's possible, but it's not worth doing.
3. I said it was a good idea all along.

ARTHUR C. CLARKE

CHAPTER

1

THE STAGES OF FI

We all know the reasons you cannot or do not *Choose FI*. You don't have to look far to find stories about young people crushed by student debt, soaring housing costs, and stagnant wages. On top of all that, investing is complicated. Against this backdrop, how can people possibly retire securely, let alone achieve FI before age sixty-five? It's easy to see why many people quickly become discouraged, and others never try.

Choosing FI becomes much easier if we reframe what FI means and how it empowers you. FI is often framed as a dichotomy: zero or one. You're either FI or you're not. You're working or you're retired.

This all-or-none thinking is the exact wrong way to frame the conversation. This makes FI seem like a far off, unachievable goal. So most people never get started. Besides, it's absurd to think that one dollar more or less in a retirement account will change everything. Yet this way of thinking traps many of us on the path to FI. Rather than recognizing the progressive freedom and power our growing wealth provides, we often get caught up in the slog. Once we realize money is just a means to an end that allows us to live the lives we want, it's easy to see that we are progressively gaining power and freedom along the path to FI.

JL Collins, author of *The Simple Path to Wealth*, has popularized the phrase "F-you money" among the FI community. He described the concept as not necessarily having enough money to retire forever, but enough to say "F-you" if needed. Having F-you money allows a degree of freedom that most don't have.

Brad told the story of using the power of F-you money to leave his job as an accountant to pursue a different path in life. Anyone can relate to his experience of being bound to the rules and regulations of an employer. Here's how he described the straw that broke the camel's back in a conversation with Jonathan on the podcast:

> "All of a sudden, we had to come in at eight o'clock instead of eight thirty, and it just ticked me off to no end. It was just that absolute garbage "facetime" nonsense that is everything I hate about corporate America. It's not the value of your work. It's not how efficient you work. It's just literally the number of hours that you're chained to your desk. And it was just such a ridiculous power play . . . you can hear it in my voice. It pisses me off to this day. And honestly, that was it. Within a couple of days, I said to [my wife] Laura, 'I can't do this anymore. I'm out.' And I walked in and put in my notice and got the heck out of there. That was a combination of A, having a growing business that I could really sink my heart and soul into and B, being well down the path to FI, albeit not at FI. But the conjunction of those two things just gave me the power to say, every other sucker has to deal with this."

But he didn't.

Leaving my safe corporate accounting job was a monumental step, and there's no way I can honestly say I wasn't scared I was making the wrong decision. I was so far along the path to FI that the easy decision would have just been to stick it out a few more years and be 100 percent sure and "safe."

But I knew I could always go back and get another accounting job, and I knew I'd always regret it if I didn't really give my best effort to growing these online businesses. I left on January 31, 2015, and started Travel Miles 101 the very next day! TM101 led me to Choose FI as Jonathan heard me talking about rewards points on the Mad Fientist podcast and that's what led to him reaching out to me in the first place. The rest, as they say, is history!

Surprisingly, Brad's story is a bit of an outlier in a community full of people who have accumulated F-you money. Having F-you money rarely means you're ever going to say those words, quit your job, and walk out after with your middle fingers in the air.

Jeremy, writer of the blog *Go Curry Cracker*, said F-you money gave him the confidence to do a better job. This confidence made his working years enjoyable and made him more valuable and highly compensated, thus shortening the number of years he needed to work. Most people he worked with were burdened with financial obligations. If you have a mortgage, a couple car payments, a family to feed, and nothing in the bank, what choice do you have when your boss asks you to do something stupid? Most people are going to say yes. Doing otherwise could put everything you have at risk. Jeremy observed that having the confidence to say, "I don't think that's the best way to do it, and this is how I think we should go forward" changes an employer's perspective of you.

Having the freedom and confidence to not go with the flow enables you to take risks that will add value to an organization. Suddenly, instead of being another pushover, you're seen as a go-getter. The power dynamic shifts when you're not reliant on your employer to provide a paycheck for your survival. The worst-case scenario is you getting fired. If you don't rely on that next paycheck to stave off disaster, the scenario is not so scary.

F-you money is a powerful concept that many in the FI community have latched on to. But it's vague. We all quantify the exact amount we need based on our individual personalities, attitudes toward money, and risk tolerance.

We need a better framework with which to quantify the stages and benchmarks along the path to FI as we track our progress and celebrate small wins along the way. Joel, who with his wife

Alexis, writes the blog *Financial 180*, discussed this at length with Brad and Jonathan when they used the framework he developed to riff on the topic.

STAGES OF FI

Joel's milestones are based on the FI community's idea that you are financially independent when your investments are twenty-five times your annual expenses. This idea comes from the 4% Rule, which is based on historical data that shows you can withdraw 4% of your portfolio on the day you retire, then continue to take the same amount, adjusted for inflation, every year going forward with little chance of running out of money. We'll examine the 4% Rule more closely in Chapter 12.

You can adjust milestones if you're taking a different investment approach and argue as to whether there should be more, less, or different benchmarks. Still, it's an interesting place to start the conversation on the way power and freedom increase as you travel the path to FI.

1 GETTING TO ZERO

The first milestone is getting to zero net worth. Having a net worth of zero, literally being worthless, may not sound like something worth celebrating at first. But for those on the standard path through life who *Choose FI*, this can be a huge accomplishment. Consider that "normal" for most people means having debt, whether from credit cards, car loans, student loans, and/or other consumer debt. On top of that, the largest expense for most people is housing, with rent or mortgage payments due each month.

For many, the next paycheck will be spent paying for past decisions.

This is a restrictive way to live. You go to work to collect a paycheck just to prevent someone from coming to repossess what you already have. There is no freedom to choose the life you want going forward.

Having no net worth is not a "worthless" goal. Whether you choose to define this as being debt free, debt free excluding a mortgage or having a net worth of zero (assets minus liabilities), hitting this milestone is important because it gives you options going forward.

I lost over a decade accumulating and then paying off debt for a degree that I'm no longer using. I didn't appreciate the time value of money. I graduated at the age of twenty-eight with $168,000 in debt.

It took intentionality, focus and a lot of hard work just to get back to zero. But I'll never regret putting in the work to get there. Getting out of debt gave me the freedom to decide where my future dollars would go rather than having to use them to pay for past decisions.

JONATHAN

2 FULLY FUNDED EMERGENCY FUND

A hallmark of financial advice for those on the standard path is to have an emergency fund of three to six months' living expenses. Having an emergency fund in cash is solid advice for most people, particularly those without other financial means to deal with the inevitable adversity of life. But what does it take to save this amount of money for someone following conventional financial advice?

If you save 10 percent of your income while spending the other 90 percent as commonly advised, you would have only accumulated about one month of living expenses after a full year of saving. It would take about five years just to fund six months of living expenses. It's no wonder many on the standard path become discouraged and wind up saving little to nothing.

Contrast this to someone who Chooses FI. Developing a high savings rate requires you to lower your monthly expenses. This lowers the bar for how much you have to save to support three to six months of spending, while simultaneously freeing up the money to save. If you can save 50 percent of your income, you will have a full year of living expenses after only one year of saving. You can fully fund an emergency fund of three to six months of living expenses within three to six months.

Quickly funding an emergency fund gives you the peace of mind that you have some cushion if something bad happens, such as an injury or your car breaking down. It also allows you to quickly start directing future savings to investments, allowing your money to start working for you.

3 HITTING SIX FIGURES

The third milestone is achieving a six-figure investment portfolio. Up to this point, you won't have had enough assets for investment returns to make a big difference on your wealth building, so you have to work hard to earn and save your way to this milestone. You should celebrate the fact that now that you've accumulated substantial wealth, it will be easier to see your money working for you, even though you still have to work for money.

According to the most recent US Census data, a six-figure net worth puts you in the top 50 percent of American households. If you subtract home equity, the median household net worth is under $50,000. While relatively rare for those on the standard path, people with a decent income and a high savings rate can achieve a six-figure portfolio quickly. A couple maxing out 401(k) contributions (limit $19,000 per person in 2019) would hit this milestone in under three years without any investment growth or employer match. Maxing out a single 401(k) gets you there in a little over five years.

If you combine a six-figure net worth with an efficient lifestyle, this is a milestone where you may have enough wealth to support two to four years of living expenses. This provides a cushion, giving you the confidence to start using F-you money without short term consequences if it backfires.

4 HALF FI

The fourth milestone is reaching Half FI. This is when your assets reach twelve and a half times your annual spending. While this is half the amount that the 4% Rule suggests you need to be FI, your journey to FI is likely more than half done. If you start with debt, it takes time just to get to zero. Then you have to save to have enough to start experiencing the noticeable benefits of compounding investment returns.

Once you've built a sizeable portfolio, your money produces substantial investment returns, which amplify the results of the efforts from you working, earning, and saving. At some point around this milestone, you will reach a crossover point. You'll begin to notice that when your investments have a good month or year, they will passively contribute more to your net worth gains than your active contributions. Passive income is what makes FI possible—this is definitely something to celebrate.

5 GETTING CLOSE

The next two milestones may occur in either order. The order will depend on the amount of discretionary spending you have in your budget. Depending on the lifestyle you desire, either may give you the confidence to start transitioning from a traditional job to a different way of life.

The first of these milestones occur when your portfolio reaches twenty-five times the annual spending required to cover all your *essential expenses* like housing, food, utilities, and health insurance. Tracking your expenses (discussed in Chapters 4 and 5) allows you to easily see how much of your spending goes to the essentials. At this point, you couldn't maintain your current lifestyle without working, but you could stop working without having to worry about going hungry or keeping a roof over your head. You could cover the basics with investment income, needing to earn only enough to cover any luxuries you desire.

The other milestone is achieved when your portfolio reaches twenty times your total annual spending. You could cover your total cost of living by drawing down 5 percent of your portfolio annually. While less safe than using a 4 percent withdrawal rate, this gives you a greater than 80 percent chance of maintaining your spending without running out of money based on historical data. It's conceivable you could leave your job at this point, with the stipulation that you're willing to be flexible with spending and/or earning if your investments don't perform well early in retirement.

6 FI

The next milestone is when your portfolio reaches twenty-five times your *entire* annual spending, which most people in the FI community use to define "financial independence." This is based on the 4% Rule. As we'll discuss in Chapter 12, this doesn't guarantee success. But considering all historical scenarios, it holds true more than 90 percent of the time. With some flexibility in spending or willingness to work to earn some income from time to time, you can now declare yourself fully financially independent. This assumes you're content maintaining the lifestyle established at your current level of spending.

7 FI WITH CUSHION

Achieving an investment value at least thirty-three times your annual spending would equate to a 3 percent annual withdrawal rate. This has never failed in any historical setting. Building an investment portfolio to this size or greater gives you security and room to increase your spending over time if desired or needed. Achieving FI with cushion allows for a feeling of abundance rather than scarcity that turns some off from the idea of FI.

PROGRESSIVE FREEDOM

You may want to create more milestones along the way. Incremental milestones have two benefits: they give you short and intermediate goals and benchmarks to keep you motivated, and they keep the growing power and freedom you have along the path to FI in the forefront of your mind. Your growing power opens more possibilities to design unique and interesting lifestyles with progressively less risk.

Seeing the power of the wealth you've accumulated can give you the confidence to abandon your "normal" job and start pursuing a different way of life. This is demonstrated repeatedly in the FI community.

ACTION STEPS

1. Define what F-you money means to you.
How much money do you need to feel secure to take more risks in your career, cut back work, or try something completely different?

2. Determine where you are on the stages of FI.
Does it make sense to continue on your current path to FI as quickly as possible? Why or why not? Explore the options available to you.

If you don't know where you are going, you'll end up someplace else.

YOGI BERRA

CHAPTER

2

START WITH
YOUR "WHY?"

Anyone who reads this book can achieve FI, and many can do it in a decade or less. You may have read the previous sentence with a bit of skepticism, or you may actually find the concept ridiculous. But take note that nowhere does it say achieving FI is easy. That's because it isn't easy! Achieving FI requires hard work—time, planning, dedication, perseverance, and a vision of realizing your effort. We profile people with vastly different backgrounds and stories, all of whom have done it or are in the process of doing it. They openly share their secrets.

Let's start with insights from Carl, who writes the blog *1500 Days to Freedom*. On the *Choose FI* podcast, Carl shared that in another interview someone asked him to share his philosophy about money. He pondered the question for several days before he was able to answer. Why was this question difficult for someone who writes a popular financial blog? He shared that it finally clicked: "The whole thing isn't really about money. It's about living the right way, and money is just a facilitator to that."

Money is an extremely valuable tool in our society, so we need to understand how to use it. However, it is vital to remember that money is not the main goal when working toward FI. This is a common theme among those who have achieved FI. Carl didn't take time to develop a philosophy of money, because it was common sense to him. But most of us do need to apply thought and effort to shift our mindsets.

J.D. Roth, one of the first personal finance bloggers who now writes the popular blog *Get Rich Slowly*, thinks everyone should define his or her personal mission as clearly as possible. He encourages you to sit down and write a mission statement and be specific about what is important to you. This gives you something concrete that will guide future actions and provide a benchmark to assess those actions.

Roth is specific about actually *writing down* your mission statement. While it is not clear how many people follow this specific advice, a very clear pattern emerges when studying people who have achieved or are close to achieving FI. Nearly all determine their purpose and mission, and it becomes a driving force that directs future actions.

The whole thing isn't really about money. It's about living the right way, and money is just a facilitator to that.

I "found" the FI framework of saving money long before I knew the formal concepts of achieving financial independence. It was a combination of many things that led me to stress saving money.

1. During a summer job in college, I was shown a compound interest retirement calculator. It blew my mind and changed my life forever.

2. I started my first job at Arthur Andersen in 2001, the "best" accounting firm in the world at the time. Due to the Enron scandal, the firm didn't exist nine months later.

3. I saw the partners at my accounting firm working seventy-hour work weeks and wasting their lives away in an office. That wasn't how I wanted my life to turn out.

4. I realized that if I stayed on the "standard" path, I would be lucky to get ten calendar days off in a row for the next forty years.

Those items created a worldview for me that rejected the normal narrative of working until my mid-sixties, so I set out to find another path. Saving money to reduce my future need to work was what I landed on.

BRAD

JONATHAN

Although I realized FI was a goal as a young adult, my path wasn't optimized for FI. I wonder if I had been exposed to this information at a younger age how that could have affected my career selection and overall outlook on life. If you can lock down enough of these principles earlier in life, you're going to end up in a wonderful financial place.

Elizabeth (Liz) Willard Thames who writes the blog *Frugalwoods*, states that as young newlyweds, she and her husband would leave their jobs in Boston every weekend and drive several hours to get into the mountains and hike. Liz told Brad and Jonathan, "our best experiences were in the mountains, just spending time together walking around in nature, not buying anything, not consuming any media." But then they had to make the long drive home on Sunday to return to work on Monday.

The simple act of realizing what made them happy began to shape their future actions and decisions. They began thinking about retiring early and moving to the mountains. Their initial vision of early retirement would put them in their fifties, a couple of decades away. But as they started to get specific about what they really wanted, they started to ask better questions. Liz shared that their conversations evolved to the point of asking, "Why don't we do it now?"

This may seem like pie-in-the sky thinking to those unfamiliar with the principles of FI, but the ability to look at the world differently than the masses is what makes FI possible. As Liz noted, they didn't have the financial resources to retire to the mountains immediately. However, she also noted, "When you have decided where you want to be in ten years, twenty years, in thirty years, it suddenly becomes very easy to line your finances up and to realize how much you're going to need to save in order to facilitate that lifestyle."

Most people drift through life and retire in their sixties or seventies because that's what they see other people doing. Liz's advice to others is to map out your goals in detail. *Then*, figure out how to make it happen. They did make it happen, retiring to their homestead in the woods of Vermont in their thirties.

For some people, motivation to pursue FI can simply mean having the freedom to slow down and experience life. Jay, a geologist and father of two young children in Houston who writes the blog *Slowly Sipping Coffee*, explained that his blog's name came from a light bulb moment that he and his wife had on a Friday off work. They realized how much they enjoyed simply having the freedom to sit down together, sip their coffee, and talk. They compared this to typical weekdays, which were characterized by running around, getting themselves and their kids ready, then grabbing the coffee while running out the door to drink alone while driving to work.

FI is not about running away from the things you hate in life. It's about running toward something.

It's being intentional about life and not just grazing through it. Once you start living intentionally, earning, spending, and investing decisions become much easier. Decisions that previously seemed hard and felt like sacrifices become automatic as they drive you toward your desired outcome.

HAVING AN AWAKENING

A common theme among those who have achieved or are along the path to FI is knowing they wanted something different from a conventional lifestyle. But before getting on the path to FI, they didn't truly believe that it was actually possible to achieve this vastly different outcome. That's why most people drift through life in what is described by Dominick Quartuccio as a "hypnotic rhythm."

Quartuccio is a life coach and author of the book *Design Your Future*. He talked to Brad and Jonathan about the concept of *awakenings*, noting life-changing events that thrust themselves upon us—like the death of a loved one, a cancer diagnosis, or unexpectedly losing a job—lead to nearly 99 percent of awakenings that lead to behavioral changes. Unfortunately, it often takes something that shakes a person to their core to be the catalyst for change.

Dominick states that taking action is the differentiator between having an awakening and simply being aware. Everyone is aware that smoking is bad for your health, but many people continue to smoke until they receive a cancer diagnosis. *Then* their awakening occurs, and they stop smoking.

An example of such a financial awakening shared on the podcast was the story of Joel and Alexis, authors of the *Financial 180* blog. Joel and Alexis were a couple of young engineers living on the Florida coast, mindlessly blowing through their incomes with no idea where their money was going. Joel pointed out, "When you get into a routine, and you do something long enough, it just starts to feel normal." They had over $100,000 a year in discretionary spending but couldn't identify where the money went. It wasn't just one thing. There were shopping trips for things they didn't really want, Amazon boxes arriving with items they forgot they ever ordered, trips they took because of family obligations or social pressure. When pressed on how they could spend that much money on unnecessary "stuff," Alexis sheepishly admitted that her thought process was, "if the payment fits, I gets."

Joel and Alexis's awakening came after Alexis was involved in a car accident. Her car was totaled, but she escaped relatively unscathed. This close call made them step back, question how they were living, and determine what was truly important to them. They started paying attention to spending and focused on buying their FI instead of more stuff. In the process, they went from saving 7 percent of their income to saving over 80 percent in one year! Once they had a purpose, change came easily.

Joel retired within five years of Alexis's accident at thirty-three years of age. Alexis, a year younger, is in position to do the same. She continues to work because she continues to find value in working. The magnitude of change in such a short amount of time was amazing. More amazingly, both Joel and Alexis agreed that they didn't have to sacrifice anything of value to achieve FI.

Joel and Alexis are a typical example of how an awakening happens. However, for many people in the FI community, awareness alone can become the catalyst for change. This is a pattern that came up repeatedly in interviews with those who are FI or are on the path.

One great example of awareness leading to awakening is the story of Noah and Becky, young professionals living in Washington state who write the blog *Money Metagame*. They noted that they started their adult lives responsibly, simply checking "all the big boxes that adults do." House? Check. Cars? Check. Investing enough in their 401(k)s to get the employer match? Check.

They shared that they were saving "a solid 6 percent [of their income] in 2014." Becky was a young neonatal nurse, and she quickly started burning out under the demands of her job. Noah and Becky began looking for how they might change their lifestyle, and they discovered the concept of FI.

Within one year, their savings rate went from 6 percent to 58 percent. While the numbers are amazing, their analysis is even more incredible for a couple that made such seemingly drastic changes. According to Noah, "our lifestyle didn't change that much, but we had a purpose for the money we were saving . . . getting us to FI." The specific strategies and tactics that can lead to such dramatic changes will be covered as you learn to spend less, earn more, and invest better later in this book.

Maybe the most dramatic awakening among the stories Brad and Jonathan collected was that of Scott Rieckens, a new father living a seemingly dream life in beautiful Coronado Beach, near San Diego. According to Scott, "I couldn't shake a nagging feeling that . . . the more success that we were finding, the harder we were working, the more would come up and the busier we would get . . . I would wake up in the morning and kiss my wife and kid, and I would head out the door to pay for this lifestyle. But I was rarely enjoying it myself."

He knew he wanted FI but had no idea how to achieve it. He was trapped in the belief that he would need some million-dollar business idea or invention. Isn't that how people get rich? He started listening to one entrepreneurial podcast after another, reinforcing this idea. Until one specific podcast episode led to his awakening. He recalled the day—February 13, 2017. On an episode of The *Tim Ferriss Show* titled "Living Beautifully on $25-27k Per Year," Ferriss interviewed a blogger named Pete Adeney, aka *Mr. Money Mustache* (MMM). The topic was how to live a better and happier lifestyle while becoming FI.

Over the next six months, Scott devoured the MMM blog and many other FIRE blogs. He began connecting with other influencers in the FI space, including Brad and Jonathan. He and his wife, Taylor, decided to uproot their family to travel the country. Scott filmed their travels, during which he met and interviewed others on the path to FIRE, eventually producing the documentary *Playing With FIRE*.

The radical change in thinking and lifestyle Scott and Taylor demonstrated in such a short period was amazing. Even more amazing is the fact that this path was there for them all along, as it is for each of you.

While filming the documentary, the crew couldn't help but see the benefits of this new way of life. Scott shared that immediately after wrapping shooting one day, he overheard a crewmember say, "I've got to get my s*&! together." Another got inspired and quickly paid off his student loans after witnessing the changes Scott and Taylor made and hearing the stories of those featured in the film.

An awakening leads some people to make dramatic life changes to pursue FI. For others, becoming aware of the concept of FI is the only change necessary to start experiencing the benefits of FI.

A great example was shared by a physician named Jeff who blogs as *The Happy Philosopher*. He felt he was burning out less than five years into his career. He recalls a conversation in which he was informed that "you need ten million dollars to retire." Conventional wisdom says it takes an incredible amount of money to achieve FI. You often hear that you need enough assets to replace 80 to 90 percent of the income that you had in your prime working years to retire.

FI is, in part, about building wealth. One way that we in the FI community think about money differently from the average person is how we define wealth. FI is not about needing an absolute amount, like a million dollars, or maybe needing ten million if you are a high-earner like the good doctor.

FI is all about the amount of money you need relative to the cost of the lifestyle you desire.

This can seem like a subtle distinction, and it may seem obvious to those who are already on the path to FI. However, for those steeped in conventional ways of thinking about money, this can be a life-changing realization. What you spend, not what you earn, determines how much you need to achieve FI. Understanding this simple concept can be incredibly empowering.

If you want a mansion, a country-club lifestyle, a new BMW every couple of years, and luxury travel at premium prices, you can do that. But you may actually need $10 million to retire. What many people realize they actually want is a safe and comfortable place to live, the ability to spend time each week with friends, the time to enjoy travel as part of a flexible and adventurous lifestyle, and a safe car to get around in. You can have the second scenario for a fraction of the cost of the first *and* regain control of your life. That awareness can lead to the awakening that brings incredible peace and happiness instead of feelings of angst and hopelessness.

This exact sentiment was shared by another physician who blogs as *Physician on FIRE*. He previously projected his future investment values and realized he was on pace to have $13 million by traditional retirement age. His awakening occurred when he realized, "Wait a second, I don't need $13 million." He didn't need to change anything he was doing. His awakening simply meant realizing his path to FI was realistic—and far shorter than he had imagined.

FIND YOUR "WHY"

Your reason for *Choosing FI* is personal; however, common themes become apparent after listening to many people who are FI or are on the path to FI. FI is about having the ability to reclaim your time and control of your life. It's about having time for family, friends, and hobbies. FI is about having flexibility. It's about having the freedom to fit in meaningful work around your life rather than trying to fit in life around your work. FI means having the freedom to pursue the options that are most personally rewarding rather than needing to chase the highest financial returns. It means having the freedom to fail on a project or in business without it leading to failure in other aspects of your life.

Todd Tresidder, author, financial coach, and educator behind *Financial Mentor* believes that what we are all really after is personal freedom. Financial freedom is simply a subset of personal freedom that allows us to pursue what is really important in life. Here are some ideas from others in the community who shared the "why" behind their journey to FI.

Remember Jay of *Slowly Sipping Coffee?* He and his wife regularly discuss the concept of a "Fully Funded Lifestyle Change." For them, FI started with the idea of having more time to spend together and with their kids rather than working ten- to eleven-hour days (plus commutes) to pay daycares, schools, and nannies to raise their kids for them. In Jay's words, "we don't want to quit work just for the sake of quitting work. We want a lifestyle change because the life we created for ourselves is way too hectic and [is] not sustainable."

Justin, who writes the blog *Root of Good*, puts it this way: "I think when you're starting out on the path to financial independence, it's really abstract . . . I take it for granted (now) because I've been retired for over three years . . . We're living like the billionaires of the industrial era. Obviously, we're not real billionaires, but we have the freedom and flexibility to really have a lot of latitude in what we do every day."

Gwen, author of the blog *Fiery Millennials*, adopted the principles of FI early in life, even before graduating college. She said, FI "gives me options which I really appreciate. It just gives me the freedom and the flexibility to do basically whatever [I] want in the future."

Tanja Hester, who retired in her late thirties while living near beautiful Lake Tahoe, writes the blog *Our Next Life*. She makes an amazing point: "We are some of the luckiest people in human history for getting to buy our way into all this leisure time and this time to try different stuff that just gets us fired up and makes us feel excited to get out of bed in the morning."

Scott Rieckens, who left his old life behind to produce the documentary *Playing With FIRE* had to convince his skeptical wife, Taylor, to join him on his dramatic FI journey to make it happen. How did he do it? He asked her to write down five to ten things that make her truly happy every week.

Taylor wrote:

- Read my baby a book.
- Listen to my baby laugh.
- Have coffee with my husband.
- Have a glass of wine at night.
- Eat delicious chocolate.
- Ride bikes with our family.
- Go for a walk.
- Spend time with our parents and our family.

Seeing the list with this level of specificity and realizing how little money it would cost gave Taylor and Scott courage, inspiration, and initiative to start down the path to FI immediately. What's stopping you?

ACTION STEPS

1. **Write down five to ten things** that make you happy on a daily or weekly basis.

2. **Determine the driving force** motivating you to seek a different way of life.

3. **Write a personal mission statement**, then read the upcoming sections about spending less, earning more, and investing better with the idea of lining up your financial decisions with your personal mission.

I hope that in this year to come, you make mistakes. Because if you are making mistakes, then you're making new things, trying new things, learning, living, pushing yourself, changing yourself, changing your world. You're doing things you've never done before, and more importantly, you're doing something.

NEIL GAIMAN

CHAPTER

3

DEVELOP A
GROWTH MINDSET

When I began writing this book, I looked for ways to distill what it means to *Choose FI*. The most successful personal finance gurus are able to simplify complex messages into simple step-by-step solutions. A perfect example is Dave Ramsey, the most widely known personal finance guru of this era. He's helped millions of people get out of debt by following his "Baby Steps." These seven simple steps are effective because they are specific and action driven.

FI is more complex than getting out of debt, although that is certainly a great starting point. *Choosing FI* is a mindset. It's about developing a framework for life more than making a single decision. As I analyzed how I achieved my financial success and compared it to others, I realized choices varied considerably. There is no magic bullet or seven-step process to follow. Despite the differences in methods employed to achieve FI, there are common patterns and traits repeatedly demonstrated by those who *Choose FI*. Possibly the most important is having a growth mindset.

Carol Dweck is a psychologist at Stanford University who writes and teaches about differences between a "fixed mindset" and a "growth mindset." According to Dweck, those with a fixed mindset believe success is based on innate ability, while those with a growth mindset believe that success is a result of continued learning, personal development, and persistence. Those with a fixed mindset tend to fear failure, which would reflect negatively on them. This leads to insecurity, masked by avoiding challenging situations to try to make themselves look good. In contrast, those with a growth mindset embrace challenges, recognizing that growth and development are results of discomfort, uncertainty, and learning from failure. Developing a growth mindset is common among those who *Choose FI*.

One of the first objections I hear when discussing FI with someone not familiar with the concept goes like this: "I would love to do that, but I don't make enough money." Another variation is, "That sounds good, but I'm not good with money" or "Investing is too complicated." These answers demonstrate two problems. The first is a lack of knowledge, which can be easily overcome through education. The second, a lack of growth mindset, is more difficult. They would be saying different things if they had a growth mindset, such as:

CHANGE   *"I would love to do that, but I don't make enough money"*
TO THIS   **"I don't make enough money to save for that yet"**

CHANGE   *"That sounds good, but I'm not good with money"*
TO THIS   **"How can I get better with money?"**

CHANGE   *"Investing is too complicated"*
TO THIS   **"What are the best resources to learn about investing?"**

Choosing FI requires genuine curiosity
and belief that you can improve,
and those two things are absolutely free.

Developing a growth mindset has been one of the most positive influences on my life in the past ten years. For most of my life, I was stuck on the fixed mindset limitations of "I'm not good at X" or "I don't have the talent for Y" or even something that's ostensibly positive like "I'm smart."

Tim Ferriss's book The 4-Hour Workweek was the inspiration I needed to start exploring new skill sets and experimenting with businesses that might fail. And fail I did! Miserably and repeatedly. But I think I failed forward with each of those businesses and learned skills from each of them that set me up for success with my early website Richmond Savers, then Travel Miles 101, and most importantly with ChooseFI.

The thousands of hours I spent on failed businesses were not a waste in my opinion, as all the information I learned about creating websites, affiliate marketing, etc. set the framework for me to be successful with my later sites.

BRAD

BECOMING A LIFELONG LEARNER

A universal principle among those who *Choose FI* is a commitment to lifelong learning. If you're not growing and learning, you're falling behind. Many in the FI community choose to lead more dynamic lives after achieving FI. Some continue in their careers, free to work on the projects they are passionate about. Others pursue projects completely unrelated to their original careers that enabled FI. Because they are passionate about these projects, some earn more money and have more impact than they did in their pre-FI working years.

A perfect example of this is the author of the blog *ESI Money*. The author, who writes under the name ESI (Earn, Save, Invest), came on the *ChooseFI* podcast to discuss growing your income. He is qualified to talk about this subject: he was president of a $100 million company, before retiring, and managed the careers of many others in the process. One of his key principles for those looking to earn more money is to "continue learning and developing your skills."

ESI practices what he preaches. He achieved FI by saving a high percentage of his salary and investing in passive index funds. He then became a real estate investor. He retired at age fifty-two. In "retirement," he's developed his blog into a viable business and purchased another successful website, *Rockstar Finance*. He essentially achieved FI three different ways, using all three investment paths—index funds, personal business, and real estate—discussed later in the book.

ESI emphasized that learning can range from furthering formal education to something as simple as utilizing time wisely when doing menial tasks, such as listening to audiobooks or podcasts. He emphasized the need to develop skills that have a financial payoff. He highlighted communication, sales, and negotiating as particularly valuable skills. Focusing on learning, growth, and development is a way of being proactive, even if you don't have a clear endgame in sight.

AGGREGATING MARGINAL GAINS

Many stuck on the standard path through life are mesmerized by celebrity culture, reality TV, and lotteries. They believe you need a big break to become rich. They can't envision a path to a better ending for their story, so they never bother trying to write it.

Those who *Choose FI* don't have a crystal ball that reveals the ending to their stories either. We start anyway. There are remarkable success stories in the FI community. Some achieve FI in less than a decade on average salaries. School teachers become millionaires. Some people retire in their forties, thirties, or even twenties! The magic that enables these extreme stories is not really magic at all. These seemingly overnight success stories don't happen overnight. They are the result of the aggregation of marginal gains.

This concept of aggregating marginal gains is explained well on the *ChooseFI* podcast by Barney, who writes the blog *The Escape Artist.* He tells the story of a cycling coach who, when asked about the key to his Tour de France team's success, replied that his cyclists brought their own pillows when traveling. On the surface, this answer sounds absurd. How can the pillow you sleep on be the difference between winning and losing among world-class athletes? In isolation, it can't. But none of the decisions we make necessarily occur in isolation.

No one has ever won a race solely by sleeping on a particular pillow, but that group of world-class athletes used the best gear, optimized nutrition, and utilized the newest innovations in training. The smallest advantage, like sleeping a little better than your competitors the night before a big race, can be the difference between winning and losing.

Every decision we make (or don't make) has consequences, many of which we could never anticipate in advance. Taking action to start moving in the right direction, even when we don't know exactly what we're doing or why we're doing it, will start providing the foundation upon which future actions begin to build.

This concept of aggregating small wins is powerful. Choosing FI is not a single choice. It's many small choices that continue to build on one another until you eventually reach a tipping point.

THE TALENT STACK

Others stuck on the standard path have self-defeating thoughts about making money that stop them from *Choosing FI*. They think they can't make more money because they don't have special talents or skills. Few people have special talents or skills. If too many people had special talents or skills, they wouldn't be special anymore. They would be common.

What you can do is develop a "talent stack," a term coined by Scott Adams, creator of the comic strip *Dilbert*, in his book *How to Fail at Almost Anything and Still Win Big*. Most of us do not have the natural ability to become world class at any particular thing. However, with effort and determination, nearly anyone can be among the top 10 to 20 percent of the population in just about anything they put their minds to. Once you develop competencies, you can connect them to create a unique skill set.

What is the story you tell yourself about yourself? I believe I'm the type of person who can learn anything. Every time I tackle something new, it starts with a question. My 2016 started with "How do I start a podcast?"

You aren't limited to just one question. Asking more and better questions and stacking the answers together makes you a more useful person.

This idea was somewhat nebulous and unformed until I was introduced to the idea of the talent stack by Dilbert author Scott Adams. The idea of a talent stack is that you can combine ordinary skills until you have enough of the right kind to be extraordinary. By stacking these diverse but complementary skills, you are able to make connections that other people simply aren't making.

In 2016, I was a pharmacist. By the end of 2018, I was a podcaster with a collection of skills in advanced personal finance, web design, marketing, coding, motion graphics, and information analytics.

Talent stacks aren't usually the result of starting with a "master plan" and executing it to perfection. They often come together in serendipitous ways. They are a result of the principles discussed earlier in this chapter: starting with a growth mindset, committing to being a lifelong learner, and aggregating marginal gains over time.

You are your own biggest investment. You can overcome many mistakes if you never stop investing in yourself.

Invest in your education and ongoing learning. Invest in your relationships and friendships. Invest in your health. Invest in becoming the best person you can be.

There are many things on the path to FI you can't control, so start by focusing on those you can. You can accumulate little wins along the way. You can develop a growth mindset, commit to a life of learning, and develop a collection of skills, talents, and interests that can be combined in unique and interesting ways.

ACTION STEPS

1. **Start each day by reading or listening** to positive material that will help develop a growth mindset for thirty minutes.

2. **Make a list of ten skills or talents** you have or want to develop. How can you combine them in unique ways to add value to the lives of others?

PART 2

SPEND LESS

Financial peace isn't the acquisition of stuff. It's learning to live on less than you make, so you can give money back and have money to invest. You can't win until you do this.

DAVE RAMSEY

CHAPTER

4

BECOME A VALUIST

rad and Jonathan ask the same six questions to end each interview on the *ChooseFI* podcast.

1. What is your favorite blog that's not your own?

2. What is your favorite blog article of all time?

3. What is your favorite life hack?

4. What was your biggest financial mistake?

5. What advice would you give to your younger self?

6. What purchase have you recently made that has added the most value to your life?

I analyzed the responses, searching for common patterns. There was only one. In response to question 2, guests repeatedly cited the January 2012 post "The Shockingly Simple Math Behind Early Retirement" from the *Mr. Money Mustache* (MMM) blog as being life altering. That single blog post serves as a wake-up call to many on the standard path, showing them there is a different way.

MMM examines the impact of your savings rate—the amount saved divided by the amount earned. In equation form, it looks like this:

Savings Rate = Savings/Earnings

It would seem that spending a dollar less or making a dollar more would have the same effect, right? Every extra dollar you don't spend or every extra dollar you earn could be applied to your savings. But, mathematically, spending less has a double effect that speeds the time to FI. Every dollar you don't spend is a dollar you can save. Simultaneously building a more efficient, lower-cost lifestyle means you need to accumulate far less to support that lifestyle with investment income, shortening the time to FI.

Once people see this simple math, they can visualize a FI lifestyle contrasted against the lifestyle they're currently living. Most people live on a never-ending treadmill of:

They save very little, locking themselves into their current lives while leaving no option to break this cycle.

In the FI community, we generally define "FI" as the point when you have investable assets equal to twenty-five times your annual expenses. This is based on the 4% Rule, which is discussed in more detail in Chapter 12. The amount you need to achieve FI is based on what you spend. For every $1,000 you spend each year, you need to accumulate $25,000 to sustain that spending from an investment portfolio. Conversely, every $1,000 you can cut from your annual spending is $25,000 you don't have to accumulate to achieve FI.

The wealth required to achieve FI is relative. A person who has a million dollars and can live well on $30,000 annually would almost certainly be able to maintain this lifestyle forever without running out of money. A person who has a million dollars but "needs" $150,000 to maintain their lifestyle would likely run out of money in a decade or less.

MMM used conservative assumptions to demonstrate that your savings rate can predict how long it will take to achieve FI. Below is a chart adapted from "The Shockingly Simple Math Behind Early Retirement" that shows how long it takes to reach FI, as a function of your savings rate.

Savings Rate (Percent)	Years Until Financial Independence
5	66
10	51
15	43
20	37
25	32
30	28
35	25
40	22
45	19
50	17
55	14.5
60	12.5
65	10.5
70	8.5
75	7
80	5.5
85	4
90	<3
95	<2

Take note that most mainstream financial advice is to save 10 to 20 percent of your income. If you follow this advice, it locks you into a traditional forty- to fifty-year career. So if you start working at age twenty-two, you can retire between the ages of sixty-two and seventy-two, the regularly recognized retirement age. In reality, most people don't save this much *any* year, and they *never* achieve FI.

The key to rapid wealth accumulation that allows FI, as demonstrated by "The Shockingly Simple Math," is to create a greater spread between what you earn and what you spend. The greater the savings rate, the faster you can achieve FI. Wise investing then allows you to grow your wealth and live off investment income indefinitely.

This leads to the three levers available to those looking to achieve FI discussed in the introduction.

1. We can spend less.

2. We can earn more.

3. We can focus on becoming better investors.

All three are valuable. It is important to understand each and have a strategy that fits your personal strengths and weaknesses and enables your desired lifestyle. Still, we have to start somewhere.

Increasing earnings and returns on investments take time— so begin by determining how to spend less. You can start optimizing your spending immediately. Spending less also offers tax advantages that further accelerate your savings rate. We'll explore this concept in detail in Chapter 6. Finally, achieving some measure of FI creates time and capital that can give you the confidence to pursue alternative career paths or investment opportunities that would seem risky otherwise. Actions enabled by your newfound confidence can throw gas on an already growing fire (pun most certainly intended).

The average American saves only about 5 percent of their income.

Those on the path to FI often have savings rates of 30 to 50 percent, with some reporting saving more than 80 percent of their incomes.

Regardless of how much you earn, you must save some of it to create the initial wealth that can grow and compound to create FI. There is great variability within that construct. FI requires relative frugality, not extreme frugality. Let's explore what that means to some people in the FI community.

LEAN FIRE VS. FAT FIRE

MMM is incredibly popular among the FI community. The blog reports an early retirement household budget of about $25,000 annually. *Early Retirement Extreme* (ERE) was the most popular FIRE blog when I was introduced to the concept around 2011. Its author, Jacob Lund Fisker, retired quickly by living on less than $10,000 per year.

Sharing examples like these with people unfamiliar with the principles of FI typically elicits one of two polar opposite effects. Some see frugality as a path to reclaiming their lives, while others think of how much sacrifice FI requires and decide it's not worth the effort.

Some people become highly motivated and start making changes immediately. Joel and Alexis of the blog *Financial 180* are a great example of this. Within a year of discovering the idea of FI, they were saving over 80 percent of their income while working as engineers. Neither made a six-figure income. An even more extreme example is a couple named Paige and Sam. They are listeners of the *ChooseFI* podcast who shared their story of saving toward FI while living in the high-cost city of Los Angeles. Both work in the LA arts community, and their combined income is well under $100,000. People working regular jobs as teachers, in military service, and as blue-collar laborers who apply these lessons become the next generation of "The Millionaires Next Door."

At the same time, others dismiss the idea of FI as requiring extreme frugality or even living in poverty. Todd Tresidder operates the financial education website, *Financial Mentor*. He calls this traditional path to achieve FI "Lean FIRE." He characterizes it as getting expenses as low as possible to gain freedom from work as soon as possible. He noted that this approach is totally valid mathematically, but it is not for everyone. According to Todd, he has spoken to many people who immediately wrote off the whole idea of FI because it seemed like too much of a sacrifice.

Conversely, he discussed the idea of "Fat FIRE," the path to FI for those who do not want to optimize all aspects of life or have life choices dictated to them by a tight budget. He points out that we can focus on increasing income while working, using investments with leverage or higher expected returns than traditional stocks and bonds, or having non-traditional retirements subsidized by income earned while doing things we are passionate about. These examples don't change the "simple math" but instead change how we work with it.

Whether you relate more to the idea of "Lean FIRE" or "Fat FIRE," you must learn to create a margin between spending and earning. It is vital to realize that it's difficult to achieve FI if you feel you're living a life of deprivation. Just as restrictive diets are effective to lose weight in the short-term, most people won't stick to them in the long-term. You can pick and choose the levers you want to pull to help spend less, earn more, and invest better. Life is about choices, and you do not have to live at any extremes unless you want to. Having said that, if you want to see any changes in life, you must take action.

IT CAN TAKE TWO

You may already understand the basics of FI, but your spouse or partner may not be on board. This is common for those on the path to FI. Jay of *Slowly Sipping Coffee* shared that this was the scenario in his household. So how did Jay and his wife get on the same page with their FI plan?

While Jay is now a big proponent of FI and writes to help others on their journey, he was the one in his house that initially needed to be convinced. His wife sent him links to MMM to convince him they could pursue a different lifestyle. His initial reaction was "no way." As he tells it, he imagined himself becoming Chris Farley's character Matt Foley from the *Saturday Night Live* skit "Van Down by the River." While Jay didn't love his job, he also didn't hate it enough to quit and live what he thought would be a life of deprivation. It took three or four years for him to get on board. It finally happened after his wife presented him with spreadsheet after spreadsheet showing him their household spending. She repeatedly demonstrated what they were spending and where their money was going. It finally clicked for him to see how much further their money would go without high income taxes, commuting costs, and daycare expenses.

My wife and I were in a similar situation. She grew up in a household that struggled with money. We got out of debt within a year of starting our careers, and from that point forward we lived a life of abundance. We did whatever we wanted with plenty left over every month to save. When I introduced my wife to the concept of FI by sharing ideas I learned from ERE and MMM, she envisioned a return to a lifestyle of scarcity. But as I demonstrated how little our favorite activities like skiing, hiking, and rock climbing cost and how we could have far more time for these activities without the need to work, she became interested. After our daughter was born, my wife became more acutely aware of how important it was to regain control of our time, and she went all in with me in the pursuit of FI.

Many couples will have similar conversations. Selling the idea of FI to a spouse or partner by presenting one or two articles from a random blogger with an "extreme" lifestyle doesn't usually work. More often, your partner will think you've lost your mind when you say you want them to embrace a lifestyle that on the surface may sound extreme. But if you can present FI as a realistic goal, you can work as a team to grow your wealth while simultaneously creating a life that allows you to pursue the things that you value most. That should make the conversation easier.

LESS CAN BE MORE

Liz, who writes the blog *Frugalwoods*, was the first guest ever on the *ChooseFI* podcast. Liz believes that frugality challenges you to put things most important to you at the forefront and let everything else fall away. She said, "When you have unlocked the magic of being content and happy with simple things in life, you're setting yourself up for success over and over again."

As hard as it may be to learn to be happy and content, it's important to remember that it's what we're all really after in the end. It's vital to remember the whole idea of your "why."

Second, Liz emphasized the importance of tracking where your money goes. She shared a common experience. After beginning her career, she and her husband started spending money with no idea where it was actually going. Her very simple and practical advice to resolve this was, "Track your expenses." She advises being specific, then taking time to analyze your spending. While it's great to know what is important to you, it's worthless if you don't align your life with those ideals. If you want to live an intentional lifestyle, you must know how to use the most powerful tool in your toolbox—money—and then align your spending with your values. This is simply not possible without knowing where your money is going.

While Liz emphasizes living a more frugal lifestyle, I identify more with the idea of "Fat FIRE." It is telling that Liz and I, on opposite ends of the spectrum concerning frugality, align perfectly on starting by finding contentment and aligning your spending with your values. However you feel about frugality, consider whether less really can be more. Are you spending money to buy a better quality of life? Or are you just buying more stuff?

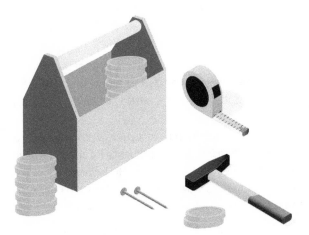

So many of us spend our lives trying to look rich and sacrifice our wealth in the process. Get a mortgage for the biggest home that you can afford then finance renovations and furniture to fill it. Cars sit empty 95 percent of the time. Basements, garages, and paid storage units sit filled to the brim with stuff that we don't have time to use because we are stuck at work so we can afford the payments. How many people never question this and are stuck on a paycheck-to-paycheck hamster wheel? I love being a part of the stealth wealth community. We're a community of people who don't wear our wealth on our sleeves. Instead, we strive to save 30 to 50 percent of our income and are willing to be slightly more intentional to do it.

JONATHAN

Let's look at another cliché related to spending money: "Money can't buy happiness." We have all heard this, and many of us mindlessly repeat it. But is it actually true?

In Chapter 2, we briefly introduced Jeff, a physician who blogs as *The Happy Philosopher*. Jeff has thought a lot about the relationship between money and happiness. He believes money actually can buy happiness; however, the relationship between money and happiness is not linear, and it doesn't work the way most people think it does.

Jeff introduced the concept of the marginal utility of wealth, the idea that the first money you spend will bring you the greatest amount of happiness. The more money you spend, the less incremental happiness you achieve. This concept may be better explained with an example:

Consider a simple dining fork. You can get a normal metal fork for about $1. Conversely, you can purchase engraved sterling silver forks for upwards of $50 apiece. Clearly, having a fork to eat your meals with, rather than trying to eat with your hands, is money well spent. But it's worth asking whether the fancier fork will give you fifty times better function or fifty times more joy than the normal fork. For most people, the answer is no. This type of thinking can then be applied to all spending decisions.

Think about the typical American family's spending. The doctors, lawyers, and executives tend to occupy the highest socioeconomic tier. Most people in that tier tend to live a similar lifestyle. Go one step down, and you will find those who make an income in that range tend to live a similar lifestyle. We don't have a formal system in our society that tells us how we should live, but we take these cues from the people we perceive to be in our socioeconomic class or the ones that we strive to be in. Most live in similar houses in comparable neighborhoods. They drive the same types of cars, wear similar clothes, and take the same types of vacations.

Does it really cost ten times more for one person to be happy than another because their income is ten times higher? In a word, no. Most people spend reflexively. As more money comes in, more money goes out in the never-ending quest for bigger and better. This is known as the hedonic treadmill. Considering the marginal utility of wealth challenges you to question this impulsive behavior and break this wealth-destroying cycle.

Understanding the marginal utility of wealth is vital to determining how frugal you can and should be. You should not be frugal to meet someone else's standards or to win a frugality contest. You should consider whether your spending truly improves your happiness. If it doesn't, maybe it's time to start investing that money to build a life that will.

The FI community runs the gamut from those who embrace extreme frugality as a virtue to those who are in the "Fat FIRE" camp and don't mind spending money on the finer things in life. The beauty of FI is that you have the freedom to determine your own values and build a plan that is consistent with those values. Many of us reject traditional labels—frugal, minimalist, or retired. You may like to spend money more than others. You may find value in owning objects that others think are pointless. You may want to work for reasons other than money. All of these things are your choice.

What ties all of us together when we *Choose FI* is that we become clear on what we want and then align our lives and finances to work toward achieving what we value. A term has grown out of the *ChooseFI* podcast to encompass all of us pursuing FI: "valuist." A valuist is someone who spends their time and money consistently with their values.

You do not have to adopt anyone else's definition of success or failure, but to gain traction on the path to FI you do have to determine what you value and then start spending your time and money accordingly.

People who *Choose FI* can seem strange to those who don't understand the concept of a valuist. Jonathan originally learned of Brad when he heard him on another podcast talking about approaching FI in his thirties. Brad also discussed using credit card travel rewards to take a trip with his wife, kids, and all four grandparents to Disney World. Jonathan was surprised the first few times he met up with Brad in person. Brad always wore flip-flops, shorts, and one of his assorted free t-shirts from FinCon, a conference for financial bloggers. Brad values travel and time with family, so he devotes time and money to those ends. He doesn't value fancy clothes, so he doesn't spend time and money trying to impress others with his wardrobe. He's a valuist.

I had a similar experience when working. My coworkers teased me frequently about my "Pap-mobile," a 2003 Chevy Malibu with cloth seats that I inherited from my grandfather when he could no longer drive. I drove that inherited car for nearly a decade while pursuing FI. Over that same period of time, I spent considerable money traveling the world in pursuit of outdoor adventures and other experiences, including major sporting events and music festivals. I value those experiences, but I don't value fancy cars. So my time and money went to travel, adventure, and experiences while still saving a lot of money by driving a crappy car. I'm a valuist.

Some more extreme—and maybe gross—examples come from Bobby Hoyt of *Millennial Money Man* and Carl of *1500 Days to Freedom*. Bobby talked of his love of boating and Carl of travel when they came on the *ChooseFI* podcast. Both men publicly "bragged" that their wives made them throw away underwear and socks with holes in them. They're not too poor to afford new underwear, nor are they too cheap to buy it. It's just not a priority to go shopping, so they don't bother. I'm not proud to admit my wife had to give me the same talk.

Being a valuist is pretty simple when you understand it. Be happy with simple things. Budget or track your spending so you know where your dollars are going. Align your spending with the things that are truly important to you.

The simplest lever my wife and I have pulled on the path to FI is that we drive old cars. My wife Laura drives a 2003 Toyota Highlander, and I drive a 2003 Honda Civic. Each has over 100,000 miles, they still drive great, and both look nice. The best part is we haven't had a car payment on each in roughly 10 years!

We've taken the $700 per month we would have spent on new or leased cars and invested that money in the stock market in low-cost index funds. We now estimate our net worth is well over $100,000 higher than it would have been if we had been making car payments all this time!

Throughout our lifetimes, this one decision will be worth well over $1 million and likely multiple millions! Just by driving perfectly lovely yet older cars. Think about how powerful that is.

BRAD

ACTION STEPS

1. **If you haven't already,** develop a system to either budget or track your spending.

2. **Sit down at the end of each month and see where your money went.** Then consider how much of your money is being spent on things that add value to your life and how much is being spent on things that trap you on the standard path without improving your quality of life.

3. **Guys: If you have holes in your socks and underwear,** go buy new ones without having to be told by your significant other. FI doesn't require us to be gross. We can do better!

80% of the results come from 20% of the causes. A few things are important; most are not.

RICHARD KOCH

CHAPTER

5

LIVE BETTER WHILE
SPENDING LESS

The Pareto Principle, or 80/20 rule, states that when analyzing any problem, 20 percent of actions will account for 80 percent of the outcome. The other 80 percent of actions will account for only 20 percent of results. If you want to *Choose FI*, a high savings rate is the ultimate force multiplier. You can apply the Pareto Principle to decrease your spending and thus increase your savings rate. There are a few factors that outweigh all the others combined. It's not rocket science. Start by tracking where your money goes, then focus on spending less on the things under your control that will have the most impact.

The three largest areas of spending we can all control to build a high savings rate are housing, transportation, and food. Here's how you can optimize spending to enable a more rewarding lifestyle faster than you could have previously imagined.

IS YOUR HOME AN INVESTMENT?

Conventional wisdom says home ownership is a great investment. Based on data from the US Census Bureau, home equity accounts for 75 percent of the average American's net worth. But those who *Choose FI* are anything but conventional.

Kristy and Bryce write the blog *Millennial Revolution*. They strongly believe that your house is not an investment. They are known as Canada's youngest retirees, an achievement they credit largely to rejecting the "cult of homeownership." Kristy and Bryce felt pressure to buy a home in Toronto, where they were starting their careers, amid a housing bubble. Prices were rapidly increasing, their friends were all buying, and they faced pressure from their families. This led to a serious case of FOMO—fear of missing out.

Amid the pressure, Kristy and Bryce stepped back to look at the math of home ownership. Many people look at a mortgage calculator to see what payments will be and stop there. Instead, Kristy and Bryce did a deep dive on the costs of home ownership—things that banks and real estate agents often brush over since their livelihoods depend on selling homes. Kristy and Bryce looked at closing costs to buy as well as what it would cost to sell in the future. They examined maintenance costs, taxes, insurance, and the expense of financing.

Bryce shares that as an engineer who is used to making objective decisions, "I was looking at all this stuff in terms of just numbers, and the numbers didn't make sense." Bryce and Kristy took emotion out of their decision, realizing they could live life with more freedom and less cost by renting instead of buying.

The rent versus buy decision is different for everyone. The key lesson from Kristy and Bryce is that math matters. The choice to own a home is one of the most important financial decisions you can make. Home ownership may make sense as a lifestyle decision, but it is rarely a good investment—unless you decide to make it a true investment as some in the FI community have.

If housing is the biggest expense most of us have under our control, it makes sense to focus on ways to start reducing expenses there. What if you could completely eliminate your housing expense? How about going a step further? What if you could turn this expense into income? Welcome to house hacking.

Todd Tresidder of the website *Financial Mentor* has lived and studied FI for decades. In response to the question, "What advice would you give someone starting out on the path to FI?" he responded: "If I could go back, I would beg, borrow, whatever to get the down payment and I'd buy that first fourplex and then I would live in it and learn all the ropes of being a landlord by living in one of the four units (and renting out the other three units) and dealing with my tenants . . . As I got that thing cash flowing, as soon as I got it working based on four units of rental, I go out and get another one. By the time you get three of those, you're done. *You're done.* It's the simplest, easiest way to achieve financial independence for somebody in their twenties."

Chad "Coach" Carson provides a perfect example of this advice applied. He achieved FI before the age of forty. His first investment was buying a fourplex and living in one of the units. He said, "By getting the rent from those other units, you can use that to pay your housing . . . That is the concept of house hacking. You're finding some way to generate income from your residence instead of just living there and having all the money go out the door." Carson added, "I challenge [you] to take away your housing payment, put that in a future value calculator, and figure out what that means for you ten to twenty years down the road. If you weren't that motivated before, I think that will start getting you more interested in the concept."

House hacking is the most powerful tool in your arsenal if you want to achieve FI in a short period, particularly for those with lower incomes and those with student loan debt who would otherwise have difficulty saving. When done well, it eliminates the largest item in most people's budgets, adds a small amount of income, and it's an investment. You can build wealth by spending less, earning more, or investing better. The decision to hack your housing allows you to pull all three levers simultaneously.

There are other options if you do not want to share your living space in the long-term. Do you have space that you could use as an Airbnb rental? Could you rent storage space in your garage, basement, or attic? Could you rent an unused parking spot? Once you understand the importance and impact of flipping the housing equation, you are limited only by your imagination to achieve FI sooner.

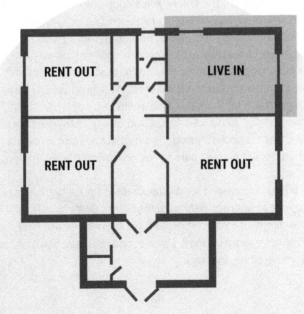

Some people may not want to pursue a house hack even after seeing the numbers. There are more options to optimize housing costs shared by others in the FI community.

Physician on FIRE reports he came out of residency in a position common to many new physicians. He could command a high income but was saddled with debt accrued during his training. Rather than adding to his debt by buying an expensive house, he worked in temporary positions as a traveling physician for two years. He and his wife lived in a half dozen different states while he worked in a variety of different practices. This enabled him to eliminate housing expenses by "living on the dimes of the hospitals and groups" he worked for. He said they would "put us up in apartments or hotels for a short period, and that way I was able to basically save every dollar I was paid. I had per diem for food, and I had lodging, and I was able to pay down my student loans while saving up for our future."

Paige and Sam, the Los Angeles couple working toward FI on below-average salaries introduced in Chapter 4, found a simple solution. According to Paige, "living with roommates was huge." This simple solution is common for college students and other young people, but there is a stigma associated with living with roommates as adults. Why is there no stigma to living paycheck to paycheck in houses or apartments that destroy wealth? The "adult thing" to do is to go out and buy or rent your own place. But there is probably nothing simpler, faster, or more practical than finding a roommate to cut housing and utility expenses.

Perhaps the easiest solution outside of house hacking is to buy or rent an appropriately sized residence. Heat-maps have shown a majority of modern homes have rooms that are never used. This costs extra in taxes, utilities, and maintenance that can be eliminated by downsizing.

STOP DRIVING YOURSELF TO THE POOR HOUSE

Transportation is another area where you can make drastic improvements in your spending. Extreme voices may say to get rid of the car and walk or bike everywhere. Doing so would accelerate your journey to FI, in addition to the obvious health benefits, but realistically, American society is designed for cars, and they are an accepted part of everyday living. Most people, myself included, are not about to give up their car to achieve FI.

In Episode 22 of the *ChooseFI* podcast, Brad and Jonathan attempted to break down the true cost of car ownership. Jonathan's game plan is to approach car ownership from the standpoint of "even if I don't win, at least I don't lose as badly." This is a common-sense approach to car ownership. Make no mistake, there is plenty we can do to lose less badly.

Look at how the average person approaches purchasing a car. Just like with their homes, many people will buy the most expensive car they can afford. More accurately, they will buy a car for the maximum dollar amount someone will lend them. According to research conducted by *The New York Times,* only about 10 percent of people purchase cars with cash on average. Similar to houses, cars come with ongoing expenses including fuel, insurance, and maintenance. It's easy to see how you can save a substantial amount of money by being smarter with your car purchase, especially if you can pay cash.

The biggest detriment to achieving FI when buying a car is that you are pouring money into an asset that loses value every day you own it and every mile you drive. Cars begin to depreciate the second you drive them off the lot. According to edmunds.com, a new car that costs approximately $30,000 loses about $2,500 of its value when you drive the first mile. It loses approximately $6,000 or nearly 20 percent of its value in the first year of ownership.

Understanding how cars can destroy wealth helps turn the equation to less of a losing proposition. Get over the idea that a car is a status symbol and accept a vehicle for what it is—an object to transport you from point A to point B. Buying used instead of new eliminates the largest amount of depreciation, which lessens after a car is five years old. It has lost about 60 percent of its initial value by then. When you buy a pre-owned car, you end up paying less and mitigate against depreciation. You don't want the cheapest car that compromises safety or nickel and dimes you with constant repairs. This is a perfect example of being a valuist—choosing the car that provides the most value for the lowest cost.

Even if you can not afford to buy your next car with cash, these practical choices can save substantial amounts of money. When you can purchase your car with cash, you eliminate the expense of financing your vehicle.

Most people who finance their car purchase continue doing it again and again, paying unnecessary expenses their entire adult lives. Even worse, others lease vehicles with this same pattern. Many get into the habit of having a car loan or lease payment, and that becomes the normal rhythm of their lives. They often think, "This car is paid off, it must be time for a new one." Those who *Choose FI* challenge this "conventional" wisdom.

EATING YOUR WAY TO FI

The third key focal point to cut spending and shorten the road to FI is controlling food costs. The cost of a meal is insignificant compared to the price of a house or a car. But you are not buying three homes or three cars a day for each member of your household. Because food is a recurring expense, small spending changes can have dramatic effects over time.

This is true in the "extreme frugality" segment of the FI community. Liz, who writes the blog *Frugalwoods*, embraces the concept of saving money on food. She believes cooking from scratch tastes better and is better for you because you determine what ingredients go into your body. Paige and Sam also espouse this principle. Sam said, "eating out is something that never really made sense to me if I could cook and eat something at home." Paige added, "I literally eat to live, I do not live to eat."

You may be surprised to hear that controlling food costs is also discussed by higher-spending members of the FI community. Remember, *Physician on FIRE* both lived and ate on his employer's dime early in his career by receiving per diems while traveling.

Ditto for Jay, the writer of *Slowly Sipping Coffee*. He is half of a pair of six-figure-earning geologists working in the oil and gas industry. He noted that when he and his wife got serious about pursuing FI, they cut out $24,000 a year in spending. He estimates, "going out to eat was at least thirty to forty percent of that."

A similar theme was heard from a Long Island native who writes the blog *Freedom is Groovy*. He said he and his wife were drifting through life without paying attention to their spending. Once they started tracking spending, they realized they were spending $800 each month to feed two people. Armed with that fact, they were able to cut the cost in half quickly.

Brad and his wife Laura set a goal of feeding their family of four for $2 per person per meal. They utilize a combination of limiting restaurant meals, meal planning, and shopping strategically. This not only allows them to eat well for little money, but it also improves their lives by increasing efficiency.

My wife Laura's meal planning has been one of the main keys to our success not only with our finances but with our health as well.

Laura loves to cook and experiment with new meals. She's always looking to optimize her meal planning to save time, money, and stress. She looks for great deals on items in bulk that she can have at the ready. For instance, she buys the "family pack" of chicken cutlets, which is normally 5+ pounds. She'll take two hours to bread and fry these cutlets and then freeze them into meal-size portions that she can take out at a moment's notice.

That time investment makes her life easier for the next few months, and she saves a significant amount of money because she's not running to the store at the last minute to buy a pound of chicken for twice the price! A little planning goes a long way.

Every week, Laura creates a meal plan. She cooks two large meals a week that will each feed our family for two nights or more. These get us through at least four nights of dinner. These two meals usually complement each other with necessary ingredients, so she saves time and money that way as well.

The entire goal is to not have to scramble at the last minute to have food for dinner each night. With a little planning and intention, she makes her life easier and less expensive, and we enjoy gourmet home-cooked meals every night of the week!

BRAD

Food is one area where my wife and I are not willing to sacrifice quality for cost. For health reasons, we choose to eat a mostly organic diet, high in produce, meat, nuts, eggs, and healthy fats and low in carbs and sugar. We eat almost no processed foods. Most people might think this is an expensive diet. And it can be. We tracked our spending very closely for a few months when we switched to this diet. We created a strategy to maximize quality and minimize costs. We began buying things like olive oil, coconut oil, nuts, and canned foods like peanut butter and beans in bulk from a warehouse store every couple of months. We buy most of our meat and produce from ALDI, a discount grocer. We use our local grocery store only to fill in the gaps for special ingredients that can't be found in the other two places. This strategy, combined with minimal restaurant meals, allows us to eat for about $3 per person per meal. While not quite as good as Brad and Laura's $2 per person per meal metric, we eat healthy gourmet quality meals every day for less than you could eat from the value menu at fast food restaurants.

Eating is a recurring expense we all have. Finding ways to optimize it will create considerable savings. It can also lead to a healthier lifestyle, which will save you money in the long run.

OTHER RECURRING EXPENSES

After exploring housing, transportation, and food, it pays to take a closer look at other areas of spending. David Bach popularized the concept of the "latte factor" in his bestselling book *The Automatic Millionaire*. He used it to demonstrate the impact of small recurring expenses over time. There's no need to give up your latte, or anything else you value for that matter, to *Choose FI*. You have the most effect on spending by focusing on your largest expenses. However, it is important to understand the impact of seemingly small recurring expenses that add up over time. More importantly, you also lose compounding that occurs over years if this money is not saved and invested.

Tracking expenses shows exactly where your money is going, allowing you to know where to direct efforts for maximum impact. First, look for areas where spending does not add value to your life. This makes it easy to save without sacrifice. Finding recurring expenses you can cut allows you to make a decision one time and reap ongoing benefits.

Most will find at least three areas to cut recurring spending while improving quality of life: insurance, cable TV, and cell phones. Those who *Choose FI* consistently spend less than those on the standard path in these areas. Let's explore them and demonstrate how spending less than those on the standard path enables a better lifestyle at lower costs for those who *Choose FI*.

INSURANCE

Insurance is a large expense for most people, so it's important to understand what insurance is, how it works, and when we need it.

Having insurance means transferring financial risks to an insurance company because it's not affordable to take on the risk yourself. This makes sense. For most people who are otherwise financially independent, a cancer diagnosis could be financially destructive. So it makes sense for everyone to have health insurance to transfer risk from the individual to the insurance company.

A key to making good insurance decisions is understanding that the insurance company must make a profit. Paying premiums to an insurance company that won't be in business when you need them makes no sense. When you buy insurance, you're making a bet you're likely to lose, and the insurance company is likely to win by taking in more money than they pay out. This is not to suggest that insurance companies are evil, and their products are inherently bad. It's just the basic math governing insurance.

This means you want to buy insurance only when you can't afford to take the risk yourself. You want to "lose" these bets to the insurance company because that means nothing bad happened to you. Instead, you forfeit your premium to the insurance company. "Winning" the bet—getting more money in benefits than you paid in premiums—means something bad happened (e.g., an injury, a car accident, a home fire, etc.), requiring you to use the insurance.

Insurance decisions can best be made by placing possible scenarios in one of four quadrants.

Low Probability, Large Impact	High Probability, Large Impact
Low Probability, Small Impact	High Probability, Small Impact

Decisions on the left side of the quadrant are relatively easy. These events have a low probability of occurring. Events that fall into the lower-left quadrant, even if they were to occur, would have a small financial impact. In this case, there's no need for insurance. Events that have a low probability of occurring but would have a large financial impact if they did are in the upper-left quadrant, such as a fire destroying your home. Because the probability is low, the insurance costs little, but its value can be great because of the potentially large impact associated with a negative event. It is a fairly easy decision to buy these types of policies.

Insurance gets more complicated in the high-probability quadrants. There is a strong rationale for purchasing this insurance because of the high probability of occurrence; however, the high probability of occurrence makes these policies expensive.

Items in the upper-right quadrant are particularly problematic because adverse events you insure against have both a relatively high probability of occurrence and potential for a huge financial impact. Medical, disability, and long-term care insurance fall into this category. These products tend to be very expensive.

Items in the bottom-right quadrant are more likely to occur but have smaller financial impacts, such as warranties on appliances and electronics and extended warranties on automobiles and other big-ticket items. These policies are small expenses in isolation, but if you need to insure many items, they represent many losing bets that are expensive in sum.

If you're living paycheck to paycheck with no financial cushion, any small mishap can represent an emergency. It's the ultimate catch-22. Those who can least afford insurance are the ones who need it most. If your furnace goes out and you have no heat, that's an emergency. You'd better buy the extended warranty if you can't afford to fix it. A cell phone you rely on for business can be a necessity. It's an emergency if you put it in the washing machine or drop it in the toilet but can't afford to replace it. Warranties to insure against these events may make sense for those trapped in this cycle, but this is a stressful and expensive way to live.

Building wealth doesn't mean bad things will never happen. It just means you'll be able to deal with more of those things with less stress when they do. When bad things don't happen, as they usually don't, you save by not needing to insure every possible negative event. These savings can then be spent on building and maintaining a better life.

As you build savings, you lessen the need for insurance. Start by attacking items in the lower-right quadrant. Eliminating warranties keeps more money in your pocket. Next, focus on items in the upper-right quadrant. It may make sense to keep these policies because an adverse event can be expensive, but you can start paying less by accepting more risk. Start lowering premiums by purchasing plans with higher deductibles.

As you progress toward FI, investments make up more of your income. Every step you take along the path to FI makes insurance progressively less necessary, allowing you to live more securely while spending less.

Most people on the standard path through life save and invest little. This makes them vulnerable to insurance salesmen who push products that claim to give the benefits of insurance with the upside of investments. Examples include whole life insurance and variable annuity products. Unfortunately, these products come with unnecessarily high costs and subpar investment returns. A simple way to save money on insurance is to keep your insurance separate from your investments. The vast majority of people who have the discipline to save and invest money, as required to *Choose FI*, are best served by purchasing simple, lower-cost insurance products and then investing the difference on their own, such as choosing a term life insurance policy over an expensive and complex whole life policy.

The only insurance that is more important to someone who *Chooses FI* than someone on the standard path through life is liability insurance. As you accumulate wealth, you can become a target in our litigious society. Fortunately, umbrella liability insurance is a relatively affordable solution. That's because it fits neatly in the upper-left quadrant of the chart. An umbrella policy covers you for liability if you're sued for more than your auto or homeowners policy covers.

It is unlikely that you will ever need umbrella insurance, which is why it generally costs so little for protection of $1 million or more. If you were successfully sued, it could have a significant impact on your finances. Buying umbrella insurance should be an easy decision.

THE ELEPHANT IN THE ROOM

Medical insurance is the one common issue that keeps people pursuing FI up at night. It is entrenched firmly in the upper-right quadrant. It's highly likely that we'll need it from time to time, and it's expensive.

Unfortunately, for those living in the United States, there is no easy answer to the challenge of obtaining health insurance regardless of your financial situation.

But being FI does offer more options than those available to most people following the standard path through life.

One option is to take advantage of subsidies provided through the Affordable Care Act (ACA) to buy medical insurance at a discounted rate. It is worth exploring the way the ACA was written. ACA subsidies make medical insurance available to low-income households who need assistance. Many people think of the ACA as healthcare reform. In reality, it's a tax law. It hasn't changed American healthcare, it changed the way people pay for it. As with most tax laws, as we'll discuss in Chapter 6, ACA subsidies are based on income.

Many who are FI can have considerable wealth without a big income. They can benefit from subsidies and buy medical insurance at steep discounts or even get it for free by structuring income wisely. Justin of the blog *Root of Good* noted on the *ChooseFI* podcast that he is able to obtain health insurance for his family of five at very affordable rates due to the way he structures his income in early retirement. As with many features of the tax code, ACA subsidies are generally friendly to those in the FI community, especially those who opt for a more traditional retirement with little earned income.

Buying insurance as an individual on the open marketplace still presents challenges. Relying on subsidies to get affordable insurance over the long-term is a gamble, especially as the law is under frequent political attack. This creates a planning challenge. Purchasing insurance can also be very expensive for those who continue to earn income rather than opting for early retirement after achieving FI.

A second option for those who *Choose FI* is to use health care sharing ministries (HCSMs) in place of traditional medical insurance. HCSMs are faith-based organizations based on the Christian tradition of helping others in their times of need. HCSMs appeal to many who achieve FI, but who are not interested in early retirement. They provide the simplicity of paying a standard share, similar to an insurance premium, without the complexity of manipulating income to receive subsidies. While more expensive than subsidized insurance, an HCSM is an affordable option with a fixed price for those who opt to continue earning substantial income after achieving FI.

HCSMs are not without their downsides. First, they are not true insurance, so they are not subject to laws governing traditional medical insurance. This allows HCSMs to deny people with preexisting conditions. Therefore, they are not an option for everyone. HCSMs also can cap the number of benefits a person may receive, which traditional insurance can not. This again helps make HCSMs more affordable than traditional medical insurance, but it also creates unique risks in worst-case scenarios.

A third option for medical care builds on geoarbitrage, which we'll discuss in Chapter 7. Many Americans who are otherwise financially stable feel trapped in their jobs by the high cost and risk of buying medical insurance on the open market. This is an experience unique to Americans. Many developed countries have healthcare systems as good or better than the US system. Almost all provide health care at lower costs than in the United States. People with the flexibility and means to travel can utilize medical tourism. This means traveling to foreign countries for non-emergency medical treatment. For Americans, this often means obtaining care as good as, or better than, what is available at home. It almost always means receiving care at reduced costs, even after factoring in travel expenses and paying for treatments out of pocket.

Like the other options, medical tourism has obvious drawbacks. It can work well for voluntary procedures ranging from dental care to hip replacements, but it is undesirable for someone with a serious or acute medical condition.

It's clear why many on the path to FI cite medical insurance as the biggest obstacle to achieving FI. All three of these strategies have flaws. While not perfect, they are options available to the FI community because of the choices we've made.

HEALTH CARE VS. HEALTH INSURANCE

Before leaving the topic of insurance, it's important to differentiate between health care and health insurance. Many people use the terms interchangeably. They're not the same thing. Health insurance, at least in the US, is primarily concerned with paying for treatment of illnesses or injuries. These impairments are treated with medication, surgery, or other interventions. Health care is a comprehensive approach that focuses on overall wellness and prevention of illness and injury.

Finding health insurance is a significant challenge for those who *Choose FI* and leave the workforce before traditional retirement age (when Medicare is an option). However, the ability to focus on your health care is one of the biggest advantages of *Choosing FI* and living a more intentional lifestyle as soon as possible.

JONATHAN

We all too often confuse health insurance with health care. There are three types of health care:

1. *Preventative* =
   Healthy Lifestyle

2. *Maintenance* =
   *Dental cleanings,
   hip replacement, etc.*

3. *Acute* = *The bad stuff
   that is out of our
   control (e.g., cancer,
   heart attack, broken
   bones, etc.)*

While health insurance largely focuses on the acute, someone on the path to FI has incredible built-in advantages when it comes to preventative and maintenance health care because we create bandwidth or space in our lives. The reduction or removal of many stressors allows us to have more time to focus on living healthier lives now, including more time to make home-cooked meals, exercise, and participate in a community.

Let me put my pharmacist jacket on: Blue Cross Blue Shield did a study that found that ten conditions are responsible for 58 percent of all reductions in health. Of that list, the top conditions are associated with lifestyle factors heavily affected by diet, exercise, and stress. Most notably, they are diabetes, hypertension, high cholesterol, and coronary artery disease.

So many people sacrifice their health for their jobs or careers, and it can be difficult to unwind thirty to fifty years of this choice.

In my original career, I was a physical therapist. I've always understood the importance of living a healthy lifestyle. I made a conscious effort to be physically active, eat reasonably well, control stress, and get good sleep.

Working a traditional job and not yet being FI is not a reason to skip workouts, eat a bunch of fast food, or pull all-nighters with regularity. That said, like most of you, I've done all of the above from time to time when life was too busy.

As I've been able to gain more control of my time, I've found far less resistance to living a healthier lifestyle. Brad frequently talks about FI as a superpower that makes life easier. This is a prime example. When you've slept well, done some physical activity, eaten a nutritious meal, and are not consumed by stress, life is simply better and easier. This creates an ongoing positive feedback loop.

It is possible, but often challenging, to find the time to do all of the things you need to do to live a healthy lifestyle when you're constantly running to keep the hamster wheel of a standard lifestyle spinning. Many jobs are sedentary, requiring the worker to sit eight to twelve hours each day at a desk and/or in a car. With a job monopolizing your time, how do you fit in regular workouts, find the time to shop for and cook healthy meals, and regularly get eight hours of sleep each night? And if you can do all that, where do you find time for other things that are important in your life?

The flip side of that is that you can design a lifestyle that puts you in control, creates space for positive things in your life, and allows you to establish habits and routines around those things. The hamster wheel of the standard path takes energy to keep pace. It is hard to escape. *Choosing FI* removes the resistance that makes it so difficult to be the best version of yourself and allows you to use that force to create a wind behind your back, pushing you toward a healthier life.

CABLE TV AND CELL PHONES

You can save substantial money every month if you veer away from "normal" spending patterns on cable TV and cell phone plans. If we assume a household could cut $100 each month on cable subscriptions and another $100 on cell phones, and stuff that $200 per month under the mattress for thirty years, they would be sleeping on $72,000 at the end of a couple decades. If we took that $200 and invested it at a reasonable 8 percent annual return, as historically provided by a passive index fund investment, it would grow to $298,071.89! This is remarkable considering data from the 2014 US Census reveals that average net worth for an American household at traditional retirement age (sixty-five to sixty-nine years old) is only $194,226. If you subtract home equity, the average net worth for those in their mid- to late-sixties is only $43,921.

Hedonic adaptation is a person's tendency to return to a relatively stable level of happiness after adapting to major events or life changes, be they positive or negative. When we have a new and pleasurable experience, it makes us happier . . . for a short while. Then we adapt, returning to our baseline level of happiness. This leads to needing the next thing, then the next, and the one after that to make us happy—temporarily. For some, this ongoing loop becomes necessary just to stay happy. This phenomenon is referred to as the "hedonic treadmill."

I was guilty of falling into this pattern with cable TV for years. My wife would get irritated when paying the cable bill and seeing little rate hikes of $2 here and $5 there. This happened every few months. She kept suggesting that we get rid of cable.

The sports lover in me was unwilling to change. How would I watch my teams? How would I function at work when everyone was talking about sports and news all day? We all have our limits, and this was mine. Having hundreds of channels of sports, news, and entertainment at my fingertips year after year was my normal. I viewed it as a necessity.

Once I got serious about FI, I started paying closer attention to our spending. Then I started challenging my wife on different things. One day, she again challenged me, saying if I really wanted to save money, I should get rid of cable. I admit that I felt palpable fear and anxiety about getting rid of this thing that was an entrenched part of my everyday life. I always had cable, even as a poor college student without two nickels to rub together. I watched *SportsCenter* every morning while working out. The TV was reflexively clicked on when I walked in the door after work. I never missed a big game.

We eventually cut the cord with the plan to get a cheaper web-based entertainment package like Netflix or Hulu. But we never did! We found something unexpected. Life was immeasurably better without this poison in our lives. Instead of watching highlights of games during my morning workout, I started listening to podcasts that enriched my life. Instead of mindlessly turning on the TV after work, my wife and I began having real conversations and became more attentive to our daughter. Instead of falling asleep to a TV show, we began reading books to our daughter. Then we modeled a positive behavior for her by reading our own books until we were ready to go to bed. Watching a "big game" now required me to go spend time with a friend or family member instead of being isolated on my own couch. This made watching the big games more enjoyable, and it made me realize how few "big games" there really are.

This pattern is common in the FI community. When Brad and Jonathan interviewed Jeff, *The Happy Philosopher*, on the *ChooseFI* podcast, he described burnout and general unhappiness with his demanding job as a physician as his original reason to pursue early retirement. Because of his high income, the path to early retirement in a short period was easier for him than for most. He just had to save a high percentage of his large income. But it still would take five to ten years to reach FI. He needed to focus on finding happiness immediately.

He took multiple actions but cited one as being particularly important to increase happiness long before reaching FI. Previously, Jeff followed the news closely and got "tied up in the gloom and doom." He watched a lot of sports, again focusing on things he had no control over. So he decided to simply stop watching. He soon found that cutting these things out of his life reduced stress greatly, a major step in emerging from burnout before achieving FI and leaving his demanding career.

Choosing FI means deciding to be different from those on the standard path through life. This requires questioning things that most people accept as normal or even necessary.

Most who *Choose FI* opt to switch from cable TV to less expensive options or cut the cord entirely. Similarly, many on the path to FI save hundreds of dollars each month by choosing mobile virtual network operator (MVNO) plans with compatible phones they match to their individual needs rather than having the newest technology and expensive plans. A couple of examples of popular MVNO providers include Cricket Wireless utilizing the AT&T network and Google's Project Fi, which utilizes the Sprint, T-Mobile, and US Cellular networks. These decisions allow the user to spend less while living happier, healthier, and wealthier lives than those taking the standard path through life.

STACKING BENEFITS

Many are turned off by the idea of frugality, equating it with sacrifice. This short-term thinking will keep you trapped on the standard path. You gain traction when you leverage these powerful tools and stack the benefits. My own story is a perfect example.

After we finished college, my wife and I started down the path most people follow. We mortgaged our first house in the suburbs with only a 5 percent down payment. To avoid private mortgage insurance, we took out a second loan. My wife worked in downtown Pittsburgh. She drove to a Park & Ride, where her car sat idle all day. From there, she rode a bus into the city, requiring a monthly bus pass. My job required driving the opposite direction to get to work. Her commute was about forty minutes each way, while mine was closer to fifty. Because we were young and just getting established in our careers, we worked long hours. With work, our commutes, and a three-bedroom house with a yard and a pool to maintain, the last thing we wanted to do was to cook. So we ate out five to six nights a week. We also went out for lunch frequently. It was easier than finding time to prepare meals.

We found ourselves working non-stop to pay for a house we couldn't enjoy, cars that were losing value while being used primarily for getting us to and from work, and unhealthy restaurant meals we ate because we didn't have time to shop and cook for ourselves.

Our existence was a textbook example of being stuck on the hamster wheel that many people keep spinning their entire lives.

After a little over a year of this, we sold our house and moved back to our hometown where the cost of living was lower. We rented a small house for three years and were able to reduce our time commuting significantly. During that time, we saved my entire salary to use as a down payment on our future home. We used the time we previously spent commuting and doing home maintenance to work on advancing our careers while also having more time for fun. We both increased our incomes, and my wife negotiated a work-from-home position. We used some of our newly found free time to develop a love of cooking, which gave us a triple benefit—a new shared activity that also trimmed our midsections and improved our bottom line.

With all the money we saved, we paid off our house in only seven years. Now, none of our money goes to rent or mortgage payments. We owe nothing to anyone, so none of our money goes to interest on loans. We don't need to earn much income to support our lifestyle. This means we have little need for life and disability insurance. Because we don't need much income, we also pay little income tax, as we'll discuss in the next chapter. We live a rich life for very little money.

When you first start your path to FI, it can be difficult to appreciate all the factors that enable you to save money, while simultaneously enabling a better lifestyle. And we've only explored the tip of the iceberg. The concepts addressed in this chapter allow you to become financially solvent and establish a positive savings rate. In the next chapters, we'll break down the concepts that allow you to live an amazing lifestyle while accelerating the journey to FI!

ACTION STEPS

1. **Determine your monthly expenses related to housing.** Include mortgage/rent payments, utilities, taxes, and upkeep expenses. What can you do immediately to start decreasing expenses? Do you need to change your long-term strategy to lower housing expenses?

2. **Determine your monthly expenses related to transportation.** Include car payments, insurance, gas, and maintenance. Calculate the amount of time you spend commuting to and from work and other frequent destinations. What strategies can you use to decrease transportation costs? Could you move closer to work and other frequent activities to decrease housing and transportation costs simultaneously?

3. **Determine your monthly expenses related to food.** What strategies can you start incorporating today to spend less money on food while maintaining or improving the quality of your diet? Could you pack a lunch? Explore warehouse stores or discount grocers? Cook in bulk? Check out the Choose FI vault (https://www.ChooseFI.com/vault/) for frugal recipes and other ideas.

4. **Google "Latte Factor Calculator."** Take a recurring expense and plug it into the calculator. Assume you could get an 8 percent return on that money if invested, representing average stock market returns. Hit calculate. Warning: If you've never done this before, prepare to pick your jaw up off the floor when you see the opportunity cost of recurring spending when compounded over time.

5. **Review your insurance coverage.** Do you have the appropriate amount of coverage for your needs? Could you save on premiums by taking on the risk of higher deductibles? Do you need more liability coverage as your assets grow? Have you shopped your rates recently? If not, do it. It is often possible to get lower rates for the same coverage simply by shopping around. You can also often get lower rates by bundling insurance products with one provider.

6. **Check your cable and cell phone bills and services.** Are you getting value for your dollars? Could you save money by reducing your TV and social media use? Or eliminating them completely? Could this simultaneously save you money and improve your life?

People who complain about taxes can be divided into two classes: men and women.

UNKNOWN

CHAPTER

PAY FEWER TAXES

elieve it or not, you can save hundreds of thousands of dollars in taxes over your lifetime. The principles I'll share in this chapter are easy to implement and 100 percent legal.

Most people are baffled by the tax code, so they don't bother trying to learn. I fit this description before I started getting serious about FI.

Brandon, the mind behind the blog *The Mad Fientist*, influenced my personal tax strategy most. He broke down the complex US tax code in a way I had never seen and developed a simple, comprehensive strategy that can be employed by anyone willing to spend a few hours learning and incorporating the concepts.

Brandon found ways to save massive amounts of money with little to no risk, rejecting conventional ideas about personal finance. Conventional ideas may work if you are looking for conventional results, but they're not right for those pursuing FI.

His strategies allow you to pay less in taxes during your working years, accelerating progress toward FI. Once you achieve FI, you can further decrease your tax burden and possibly eliminate income tax entirely. This combination can allow you to cut back or stop working completely. Are you starting to get interested in tax planning?

What I love about FI is that it leads you to think differently and challenge all your assumptions. This is especially true when it comes to taxes! My wife and I are both CPAs, so we have a solid understanding of taxation, but the many benefits of looking at optimizing your taxes through a FI lens weren't even obvious to us!

BRAD

We need to lay some groundwork before we dive deeper into the stories and strategies of *The Mad Fientist* and others in the FI community. If you cringe at the thought of taxes and feel this topic is too complicated, bear with me. I was once like you. This is a topic that deserves your attention and understanding. It really is less complicated than you may imagine. Let's start with a few basics.

This section is specific to readers in the United States using laws and tax rates as of 2019. Numbers will change over time, but the principles likely won't. Readers from most countries will recognize similar themes and structure, but you'll need to apply them to the specific laws that govern you. Consult an accountant or review the current tax codes before doing any specific planning in case any details have changed since the publication of this book.

You must first understand how income is taxed in the United States. Not all earnings are taxed at the same rate. For example, in 2019, a married couple without children filing their taxes jointly pay no tax on their first $24,400 using the standard deduction. They can earn another $19,400 and pay only 10 percent income tax on that amount. The next $59,550 is taxed at 12 percent. As you earn more, rates of taxation increase incrementally to 22 percent, 24 percent, 32 percent, 35 percent, and finally 37 percent for the highest earners. These percentages are known as marginal tax rates. Your last dollars earned will be taxed at their marginal rate. The average rate of taxation is your effective tax rate. The effective rate is calculated by dividing the total tax paid by your total earned income.

Let's demonstrate with a hypothetical scenario.

A couple, Amaya and Greg, earn $200,000. They do not utilize tax-advantaged investment accounts, so they pay $30,493 in federal income tax. A visual is helpful to see how we get that number.

Earned Income	Income Tax Rate	Income Tax Owed
$24,400	0% (Standard Deduction)	$0
$19,400	10%	$1,940
$59,550	12%	$7,146
$89,450	22%	$19,679
$7,200	24%	$1,728
$200,000 (Total Income)	Effective Rate = 15.2%	$30,493 (Total tax due)

The second thing to understand is that the high savings rate required to achieve FI allows flexibility for tax planning. This means you can defer taxes on a percentage of your income, enabling substantial tax savings in the year money is earned. Consider a simple math example of someone with a 22 percent marginal tax rate and $10,000 to invest. If you contribute $10,000 into your 401(k)*, you automatically save $2,200 on your federal tax bill in that year. The key is also to invest that $2,200 of "free money" to keep your savings snowball growing.

*Throughout this chapter, we use the term 401(k) to refer to work sponsored retirement accounts, because it is the most common option. You may work for an employer that provides a 403(b), Simple IRA, or be a federal employee with access to the Thrift Savings Plan. The self-employed may also utilize SEP IRAs or Solo 401(k) accounts. There are differences in contribution limits and other technical details between these plans, but the basic premise and strategies we describe are applicable to any of them.

A foundational part of our message at ChooseFI has become "control what you can control"—your current tax rate is part of that. Therefore, we advocate deferring as much as possible in your 401k and Traditional IRA because it lowers your income tax liability today.

Now we'll apply this concept to our example couple earning $200,000. What if they employed the strategies discussed in the last chapter to reduce their annual spending to only $40,000? They could save the maximum amount allowed in two 401(k) accounts ($19,000 per person in 2019) and a health savings account (HSA) ($7,000 per family in 2019). This means they could avoid paying taxes on $45,000 of their most heavily taxed money while also being able to invest inside taxable and Roth accounts. Removing $45,000 lowers taxable income from $200,000 to $155,000. Their marginal tax rate, the highest rate at which they are taxed, decreases from 24 to 22 percent. Far more importantly, their effective tax rate, the percent of tax they actually pay, decreases from 15.2 to 10.2 percent. This translates to a tax savings of over $10,000 in a single year. Let's break it down again.

Earned Income	Income Tax Rate	Income Tax Owed
$45,000	0% (Tax Deferred Saving)	$0
$24,400	0% (Standard Deduction)	$0
$19,400	10%	$1,940
$59,550	12%	$7,146
$51,650	22%	$11,363
$200,000 (Total Income)	Effective Rate = 10.2%	$20,449 (total)

If you spend every dollar you earn, you lose the ability to defer taxation of income and control when and at what rate it is taxed. Developing a high savings rate works greatly to your advantage when tax planning. This is a great incentive to lower your cost of living and develop a high savings rate (see Chapter 4). Lower expenses give you greater flexibility to leverage tremendous tax savings, speeding your time to FI.

Tax-deferred retirement accounts and HSAs offer a rare opportunity to get a break on taxes. Take advantage of it. In addition to the stated tax advantages, using your 401(k) or other work-related retirement accounts have several other advantages. A big one is that many employers will match a percentage of your contribution. This is totally free money that is added to your tax-deferred investments and does not count against the limit you can contribute. When someone offers you free money, take it! An additional advantage of utilizing a 401(k) is that contributions are taken out of your paycheck before you ever see the money. This forces you to pay yourself first and eliminates the need for the willpower to do anything to save and invest money on a month to month basis. Do it! Future you will thank you someday.

When I was paying off my student loan debt, it was always a source of frustration that it's difficult to pay off the debt in any tax-advantaged way. I would read articles of people who got their effective federal tax rate close to zero while saving $30,000 to $50,000 per year. Because I was paying down debt, I didn't have the same ability. Getting rid of debt gives you freedom and flexibility, which allows you to take full advantage of the tax code and control your tax rate.

JONATHAN

TIMING STRATEGIES

Conventional thinkers say you are *not really* saving all this money in taxes. You are simply deferring taxation and will have to pay later. Brandon, *The Mad Fientist*, says this does not apply to those who choose to pursue FI, particularly when you retire at a young age. He believes we should defer taxation on as much of our income as possible during our working careers. Then we pay these taxes over long periods at lower tax rates, possibly as low as 0 percent.

A basic understanding of marginal and effective tax rates as laid out in the previous section is mandatory to implement his strategies, which have become conventional wisdom in the FI community. You eventually have to pay taxes on tax-deferred savings. However, you can take money that would have been taxed at rates as high as 37 percent and pay it later at rates as low as 0 percent, creating an amazing opportunity for tax rate arbitrage! This works because a person or couple with a high savings rate will defer earned income that would have been taxed at higher marginal tax rates in the year earned and later pay that income tax at a much lower effective tax rate due to the low-cost lifestyle they built that enabled their savings in the first place.

Returning to our hypothetical couple, Amaya and Greg shifted taxation of $45,000 that would have been taxed at 22 to 24 percent. This saved them $10,044 in the year they took this action. This also allowed them to invest the tax savings where it could go to work for them for years or even decades rather than watching the money disappear to the tax man.

If they took this same $45,000 and used it later to support themselves in retirement when they had no other income, their taxes would be $2,084. This is a real tax savings of $7,960. No fancy tricks and no advanced knowledge are required. Let's look at it in table form again.

Earned Income	Income Tax Rate	Income tax Owed
$24,400	0% (Standard Deduction)	$0
$19,400	10%	$1,940
$1,200	12%	$144
$45,000	Effective Rate = 4.6%	$2,084 total

Having a high savings rate allows for dramatic tax savings in the year money is earned, accelerating the journey to FI. This enables an arbitrage opportunity, shifting taxation of those dollars from high rates in the year they are earned to much lower rates when you don't earn income.

TAXATION OF INVESTMENTS

Timing strategies are just one part of the tax savings available to those who *Choose FI*. The next principle is that the IRS does not treat all income equally. Earned income from a job is taxed most heavily. The more you earn, the less friendly the tax code is. As we shift from earned income to income generated by investments, the tax code shifts further in our favor.

For now, let's focus on paper investments consisting of stocks and bonds. We favor holding these investments in low-cost index funds or exchange-traded funds (ETF) in large part because they are simple and tax friendly. (We'll cover passive index investing in detail in Chapter 12). Once you understand these concepts, we can expand them to other investing options. Options include investing in your own business (Chapter 13) or investing in real estate (Chapter 14). Each of these paths produces even more options to limit taxes, allowing you to keep more of the wealth you create.

Most investment income (e.g., qualified dividends and long-term capital gains) is taxed at only three rates: 0 percent, 15 percent, and 20 percent. The tax rate is 0 percent for those with incomes at or below the 12 percent marginal tax rate. Interest and short-term capital gains are taxed at your marginal tax rates. This tax structure gives further incentive to learn to live well for less, allowing you to pay little or no tax on investment income.

To this point, we've focused on the advantages of investing in tax-deferred vehicles. Tax-deferred accounts allow you to defer income in the year it is earned, allow investments to grow without taxation, then pay taxes when the money is taken from the account. Tax-deferred saving is advantageous for those pursuing FI, particularly if you anticipate being in a lower marginal tax bracket when you will need this money.

But there are advantages to Roth accounts as well. Roth accounts require you to pay tax in the year money is earned. Investments in these accounts then grow tax-free forever and are withdrawn without further taxation.

After filling up tax-deferred savings options, such as work-sponsored retirement accounts and health savings accounts, those saving a lot of money in a given year still have the opportunity to utilize a Roth IRA. Low-wage earners paying little or no income tax may benefit by using a Roth IRA rather than tax-deferred accounts. A Roth IRA allows you to contribute after-tax dollars. That money then grows forever without annual taxation of dividends, interest, or capital gains. Withdrawals are tax-free after age 59 and a half. An additional benefit is that *contributions* can be accessed prior to age 59 and a half without penalty. A Roth IRA allows for tax diversification and more flexibility when developing strategies to withdraw money.

FRUGALITY, FLEXIBILITY, AND WEALTH

Let's reinforce a concept that should now be apparent. There are two common features that those who *Choose FI* have that allow tremendous tax saving opportunities:

1. A relatively low-cost lifestyle creates a margin between earning and spending which allows using tax-advantaged investing accounts.

2. Investments create tax-friendly income, providing more margin and flexibility.

People trapped in the conventional lifestyle of spending all they earn have little margin and little accumulated wealth. This limits tax planning options. This is common to those following the standard path through life. Average people complain about the tax code, but those who *Choose FI* take the time to understand it, then use it to their advantage.

FINDING THE SWEET SPOT

If you are hung up on the idea of having to live a low-cost lifestyle, it is worth quantifying what that means with regards to the tax code. The sweet spot for tax planning is to get taxable income in the 12 percent marginal tax bracket. This is possible once you no longer need a large income to support your living expenses and save toward FI, opening you up to many options.

Keeping taxable income in the lowest marginal tax brackets produces a low effective tax rate, and it allows most investment income to be taxed at 0 percent. Without doing anything to lower your taxable income, a married couple with no kids could earn or take distributions from tax-deferred accounts up to $103,350 utilizing the standard deduction in 2019, meaning $0 tax liability on most investment income, before reaching the top of the 12 percent marginal tax bracket.

According to the most recent US Census data, the average American household income is $59,039. Being able to live on over $100,000 with little tax liability allows you to live far better than most, even if your spending looks like everyone else's. Optimizing spending on housing, cars, and food and having less need for insurance means those who *Choose FI* have a lower base cost of living. This allows a large portion of spending to go toward items like travel, entertainment, charity, or anything else you value.

Some people may desire a lifestyle of higher spending. You could spend well over $100,000 each year by supplementing taxable income. Saved cash, cost basis on investments (the amount contributed before growth), and money from Roth IRA accounts can all be withdrawn and spent completely tax-free. This allows you to use income from a variety of sources to further limit your tax burden. Lower spenders can utilize these sources of income in combination with tax-deferred income up to the standard deduction to completely eliminate income tax once they achieve FI.

You can use a combination of strategies to pay less tax while working toward FI. You will pay little to no income tax once you choose to cut back paid work. This crushes one of the largest expenses most people have throughout life with absolutely no sacrifice . . . unless you enjoy paying taxes.

PART-TIME WORK AND SEMI-RETIREMENT

The concepts discussed thus far focus on a traditional work career followed by retirement with little to no income. We started there because this makes tax planning easier conceptually. However, *Choosing FI* enables you to enjoy a flexible lifestyle. Let's look at tax strategies dealing with non-traditional approaches to work and retirement.

A common theme with people who discover FI is burnout from demanding careers that dominate their time. Even people in careers they enjoy sometimes burn out. But what if you worked fewer hours? People assume that if you work 25 percent or 50 percent less, your income goes down proportionally. This is not necessarily the case. Referring back to the example earlier in this chapter, the first dollars you earn are taxed favorably, but the last dollars you earn are taxed more heavily. This is particularly true of high earners. The blogger *Physician on FIRE* decided to cut his shifts by 40 percent to ease into retirement. If he worked any more than that, he would have lost 50 percent of subsequent earnings to taxes. Having the flexibility to work less allows you to earn money more efficiently. Hopefully, decreasing hours makes work less demanding and therefore more enjoyable.

I witnessed this in my own house. My wife decided she didn't want to return to full-time work after the birth of our daughter. At first, we questioned this decision because we assumed we would have to work longer to save enough to retire. When we ran the numbers, we realized we didn't lose much by eliminating dollars earned at our highest marginal tax rate. The combination of leveraging a part-time schedule and negotiating a work-from-home, location-independent position led her to like her job so much she decided she didn't want to retire. This actually gave me the confidence to leave my job even sooner and with more security than I otherwise would have.

Mini-retirements are another option. We introduced Noah and Becky, who write the blog *Money Metagame*, in Chapter 2. Becky is a neonatal nurse who found herself burning out on her demanding job. Only a few years into their careers, they were not in the position to retire and walk away from paid work forever. Fortunately, they had reached a level of FI that allowed them to step away from work for what they described as a "gap year." They decided to start their year away from work in January. Because taxes accrue on an annual basis, this gave them a full calendar year with almost no income. This time also gave them an opportunity for creative tax planning. They were considering options like a Roth IRA conversion, described in the next section is a year when they would have little to no income.

Once you understand basic tax planning concepts and combine them with the flexibility FI offers, abundant tax planning options become apparent. The fun part becomes designing a lifestyle that maximizes fulfillment and satisfaction while matching it to strategies that allow you to do it while paying less tax.

The topics already discussed may have your head spinning if you're new to the idea of tax planning and the opportunities available to those who Choose FI. If so, that's OK. Spend some time on this section and digest it. This gives you the key information you need to get started. Understanding that you can control your taxes and that it is as simple as contributing money to tax-advantaged retirement and health savings accounts is enough to allow you to start developing an actionable strategy today that can save you thousands of dollars a year on taxes.

In Chapter 5, we introduced the Pareto Principle, the 80/20 analysis, and applied it to developing a high savings rate. This same principle can be applied to tax planning. The strategies already outlined provide the 20 percent of actions that will give you 80 percent of results to minimize income taxes.

Many in the FI community have built on these basic tax strategies to further lower their tax burdens while working. They then can eliminate income taxes in retirement. This is masters-level tax planning. Don't worry if everything doesn't make sense yet. You can always come back and revisit these more advanced concepts once you've mastered the basics. For those hungry for more, let's explore some of these advanced ideas and techniques.

NEVER PAY TAXES AGAIN

Jeremy writes the *Go Curry Cracker* blog. One of his articles, "Never Pay Taxes Again," sounds like internet clickbait, but for those who choose early retirement with little or no earned income, it is simple, practical, and actionable advice. He explained how to eliminate income tax in four easy steps. His first two steps have already been discussed. First, choose leisure over labor. Second, learn to live well for less. He then introduces two technical topics that are worth exploring further.

The first is leveraging Roth IRA conversions. These conversions allow you to take money from tax-deferred retirement accounts, pay income tax on this money at low rates in years when earned income is low, then convert the funds to Roth accounts where they will never be taxed again.

You avoid taxation of income in the year money is initially earned by deferring taxation. That money grows tax-free for years until doing the conversion. These funds are taxed at the time of the conversion, when you are not working. Because earned income is low when doing the Roth conversion, taxes are paid at rates as low as 0 percent for money below the limit of the standard deduction. This money is then rolled into a Roth IRA account where it again can grow tax-free until the money is withdrawn tax-free. This "Roth Conversion Ladder" can be optimized step by step over the years by an early retiree. This allows complete elimination of taxation of this money.

Other techniques described by *Go Curry Cracker* include harvesting capital losses and harvesting capital gains in taxable investment accounts. These counterintuitive techniques can also be leveraged on the more basic ideas described earlier.

Tax loss harvesting is a commonly known tactic that many in the FI community take advantage of. It is utilized when you want to lower taxable income in a given year by purposefully realizing investment losses in taxable accounts. When markets go down, you sell off investments in taxable accounts. This goes against conventional wisdom that says buy low and sell high. You want to sell low in this instance because you will then buy a similar investment immediately. Thus, you stay invested and experience the investment upside when markets go back up, but you've locked in a paper loss that lowers your tax bill in the year you made the transaction. You must be careful to buy an investment that is similar, but not identical to the one you sold. If the replacement is not similar enough, you add tracking risk. This is the risk that you don't experience the full rebound when markets go back up. If you buy an investment identical to the one you sold, it violates the IRS "wash sale" rule, which aims to limit this practice.

Tax gain harvesting is uncommon but valuable to those who are FI and are earning little or no income in a given year. It is very simple. In this case, you sell off as much of your taxable investment portfolio as possible each year where you have unrealized gains while limiting recognized gains to a level that they don't push you above the 12 percent marginal tax bracket. Up to that point, investment gains are taxed at 0 percent.

Conventional wisdom says not to sell investments until you must to avoid unnecessary taxation. However, those who are FI can find themselves in unique situations. Using tax gain harvesting requires paying taxes on the event you create by selling investments. The tax is conveniently paid at a rate of 0 percent. After selling off investments and triggering this taxable event, you can immediately repurchase the identical investments in the same quantities. The advantage is that if you sell these investments later, you will have stepped up the cost basis, or purchase price, of your investments. Only future gains from this point will be taxed. You don't have to worry about switching investments to avoid a "wash sale" because you already paid (at a rate of 0 percent) your taxes on these recognized gains.

Using advanced strategies to pull money out of these retirement accounts such as the "Roth IRA Conversion Ladder" allows you to potentially pay little or no tax down the road when you want to withdraw it. But who outside of the FI community has ever heard of this?

Tax gain harvesting is another one that probably never would have crossed my desk in a traditional accounting job because it is so counterintuitive: who seriously wants to create taxable income? Answer: someone in the FI community who is controlling their tax rate and knows they'll pay $0 in tax on their capital gains!

BRAD

SPECIAL CIRCUMSTANCES

The next section won't apply to all readers but can be valuable if you are in a position to take advantage. It also demonstrates examples of what is possible for those who think differently.

457(B) ACCOUNTS

Some state or local government employees have access to 457(b) accounts. These accounts are available to school teachers, police officers, firefighters, and other civil servants. They function similarly to 401(k) or 403(b) accounts, allowing a worker to defer taxation on earnings. They also have two distinct advantages. Contributions can be made to both a 457(b) account and other work-sponsored accounts in the same year, allowing a worker to double their tax-deferred contribution for that year. The other great advantage to a 457(b) account is that unlike most other retirement accounts, money can be taken from a 457(b) account before age fifty-nine and a half without paying a penalty. This creates more flexibility once you reach FI.

Gerry Born, who writes the blog *Millionaire Educator*, is a public school teacher, as is his wife. They utilized these accounts to all but eliminate income taxes while saving toward FI. Doing so gave them each access to multiple retirement accounts to defer income, allowing them to pay a grand total of $190 in federal income tax in 2016 while saving nearly $100,000 of their two public school teachers' salaries.

Another great example is Justin, who writes the blog *Root of Good*. He was able to use similar tax-deferral strategies, paying $150 income tax on his household's $150,000 earnings, an effective tax rate of 0.1 percent. He used a combination of the above-outlined strategies, making the maximum contributions to all available tax-deferred accounts. This included utilizing a 401(k) and 457(b) while also contributing 6 percent of his salary to his pension. His wife also made the maximum allowable contributions to her 401(k), Dependent Care Flexible Spending Account, and HSA. They then utilized tax loss harvesting to further lower taxable income. All of these efforts led to a low recognized income, allowing them to contribute to tax-deductible IRA accounts, which they also took advantage of. These combined efforts allowed his family to essentially eliminate taxation of their incomes while working. This money can then be accessed after achieving FI at low rates, possibly paying no tax at all.

BACKDOOR AND MEGA BACKDOOR ROTHS

Not everyone has access to a 457(b) account to defer large amounts of money. Once you max out available tax-deferred investing, consider contributing money to a Roth IRA. The contribution limit for a Roth IRA for 2019 is $6,000 per person. Roth accounts have income caps above which you are not eligible to contribute. In 2019, the phase-out starts for individuals earning more than $122,000, and you can't contribute at all if you make more than $137,000. For a married couple, the amount you may contribute starts to decrease with incomes over $193,000, and you can't contribute at all if income is greater than $203,000. That is where most people stop. But those who *Choose FI* are not most people.

Physician on FIRE shared that after maxing out all of his available options for tax-deferred saving, he still wanted to contribute to a Roth IRA. He used what is referred to as a "backdoor" Roth IRA contribution because of his high income as a physician. A backdoor Roth requires making a contribution to a non-deductible IRA account, then immediately converting it to a Roth IRA where it can grow tax-free and be withdrawn without taxation. You accomplish the same thing as a direct Roth IRA contribution but have to add a step to put the money in through the "backdoor" to sidestep the income limit. *Choosing FI* sometimes means solving a problem differently.

Fritz Gilbert writes the blog *The Retirement Manifesto*. He goes one step further and utilizes the "Mega-Backdoor Roth," another option some can use if their employer's retirement plan allows it. In this scenario, after maxing out a tax-deferred contribution to a retirement plan, you make an additional non-deductible contribution to your 401(k). These after-tax contributions that would otherwise be invested in taxable accounts can then be converted to a Roth IRA where growth and distributions will never be taxed again. This allows you to contribute tens of thousands of additional dollars each year to tax-advantaged accounts, putting the "Mega" in "Mega-Backdoor Roth."

CREATING YOUR OWN ADVANTAGES

We've focused on tax advantages available to people working as employees and investing in traditional paper investments. People who *Choose FI* tend to have an entrepreneurial mindset. When you develop a small business or invest in real estate, you open up even more possibilities to grow your wealth while paying less tax. We will explore some alternative investing options later in the book.

ACTION STEPS

1. **Explore your company's retirement plan.** Do they offer an employer match of your contributions? If you're not already doing so, start contributing at least to the level of the match to claim your free money.

2. **Are you eligible for an HSA?** If so, explore your investment options and consider contributing the maximum allowable amount for the year.

3. **If you are self-employed,** research the different tax-advantaged retirement accounts available to you.

4. **As your salary increases and/or you save more money,** make it a habit to redirect those savings to tax-advantaged accounts until you are able to max out all of the tax-advantaged savings opportunities available in your particular situation.

Travel is fatal to prejudice, bigotry, and narrow mindedness, and many of our people need it sorely on these accounts.

MARK TWAIN

CHAPTER

7

SEE THE WORLD

Choosing FI requires making many smaller sub-choices. Those who *Choose FI* become valuists, aligning spending with values. We create high savings rates and learn to grow money by investing wisely. But one choice outweighs all others.

You must first make a decision to think differently than those who follow the standard path in life. The FI community demonstrates this clearly by placing value on travel. People who take the standard path tend to view travel as a luxury. As such, they approach it in one of two ways: some view it as a luxury they can't afford, so they never leave their little corner of the world to see what else is out there, while others embrace the idea of luxury and pay premium costs for vacations.

A consistent theme in the FI community is that travel is vital. We find ways to travel more while spending less than most. Many have discovered their travels don't slow the path to FI. We look at travel as an investment that can yield new insight and perspective, actually speeding the path to FI. The desire to travel and willingness to be mobile are among the most powerful tools available to those who *Choose FI*.

TRAVEL MORE, SPEND LESS

Jonathan and Brad met after Jonathan, while trying to learn how to save money while traveling, heard an interview with Brad on another podcast. After discovering they both lived in Richmond, VA, Jonathan reached out to Brad, initiating the friendship that led to the *ChooseFI* podcast.

My introduction to Brad occurred in a similar way about a year earlier. I became interested in using credit card travel reward points and wanted to learn more. I reviewed Brad's travel course for a freelance writing assignment. I fell in love with the idea and reached out to him.

Many people never establish a high savings rate because they view saving money as too much work, effort, and sacrifice. Not only does the FI community reject the idea of saving as a sacrifice, but many have also turned it into a game. The name of Noah and Becky's blog, *Money Metagame*, came from the idea of turning personal finance into a game. Becky said using credit card reward points is what got it all started for them.

This idea of gamifying travel plans to maximize rewards is a popular topic in the FI community. The flexibility many who *Choose FI* have built into their lives can be leveraged on top of generous credit card travel rewards. Many in the FI community use credit card rewards to regularly travel for pennies on the dollar in a quest to explore the world at minimal cost.

*When my daughters fell in love with Disney's **Frozen**, I knew a trip to Walt Disney World was in our near future. But I realized that was going to cost us over $4,000 for flights, hotels, and park tickets! That just wasn't palatable, so I looked for a better answer. That's when I found the incredible world of credit card travel reward points!*

I quickly realized my wife and I could open up targeted credit cards to get our entire trip for nearly free. It took us about eighteen months to earn all the necessary points, but it was well worth it! We stayed on-site at the Walt Disney World Swan and Dolphin Resort and got four direct flights to Orlando and our park tickets for a combined cost of around $150. This was a $4,000+ savings just with a little planning, organization, and smart credit card habits.

My wife is from Zimbabwe. Although we live in the United States, we made a commitment to each other that traveling to visit her family would be a priority. Initially, we planned on setting aside $4,000 in our budget so we could see them every two years. But learning about travel rewards changed all of this. Suddenly, we were able to travel each year for very little cost. By simply changing my purchasing process and looking at the problem differently, my wife and I were able to essentially travel the world for free.

Using credit card reward points is an advanced technique, an additional tool for those already on the path to FI. This should be incorporated once you are out of debt, have your spending under control, and are able to make the full payment on the card each month, so you're not paying high interest rates to a credit card company.

Vacation can be a great way to escape the stress of everyday life. Using reward points can also help you prepare for anything life throws at you. These can be bad times, like wanting to visit a sick or dying relative in a distant location, or good, like attending the wedding of a friend on a tropical island. In either case, a bank of travel reward points provides more flexibility and less financial stress than someone on the standard path.

Living a better quality of life while decreasing spending is reason enough to learn strategies and techniques for using credit card travel rewards, but traveling to new and interesting places can have far more benefits. Leaving the comforts of home can lead to new perspectives that can change your life.

A NEW PERSPECTIVE

Most people see the world the same way as the people who surround them. We get trapped in echo chambers, and the ability to think independently becomes grossly underdeveloped.

Traveling exposes us to different people, places, cultures, and new ways of looking at the world.

This is invaluable for those looking to *Choose FI* and take a different path.

Canadians Bryce and Kristy of the blog *Millennial Revolution* shared a story which illustrates the myopic viewpoints held by many. When Bryce and Kristy told their family they were going to spend a few months living in Mexico, they were met with resistance. The reaction was "Oh God! You're going to get killed!" because this was the impression of Mexico their families got from news reports. But Bryce and Kristy weren't dissuaded. They went and stayed with an Airbnb host in Cancun. They became friends with their host, who was a scuba instructor and shared their passion for diving. One evening, Bryce and Kristy mentioned they received a PADI diver certification in Thailand. Their host stopped and said, "Oh gee, Thailand, I hear it's dangerous." The irony was not lost on Bryce, who concluded that everyone thinks the place they live is safe and the rest of the world is dangerous.

Bryce and Kristy realized this attitude is not limited to safety. As they traveled from place to place experiencing different cultures, they witnessed people living their lives in different ways. Bryce realized some of his long-held assumptions are not universal. He also said traveling opened his eyes to the fact there are many ways to live beyond what we think of as normal.

This was echoed by Brandon Pearce, who writes the blog *Pearce on Earth*. Brandon went from working as a call center technician to a location-independent entrepreneur. He started a software business serving music teachers. This allowed him to have a nomadic lifestyle, traveling the world with his wife and three children. He said, "I think the most powerful thing for me about travel is, or at least in the beginning stages was, just realizing that my way of doing things the way I've always done (them) isn't necessarily the only right way to do things." He added, "There are so many amazing, wonderful people out there doing things, thinking things, and believing things completely differently from me, yet they exude the same genuine humanity that I possess."

I can relate to these sentiments. My wife and I began traveling extensively once we finished college. Our travels revolved around chasing our passion for outdoor adventure. This took us off the beaten tourist paths to areas plagued with poverty, including rural Mexico, Ecuador, and Tanzania.

An experience we had hiking up Mount Kilimanjaro in Tanzania changed our perspective. Tourists are required to use guides and porters to obtain a permit to climb Mount Kilimanjaro, ensuring jobs for locals. The guide service sent a packing list to prepare us for the trek. They recommended a sleeping bag with down or synthetic stuffing warm enough for sleeping in 0°F temperatures. Every day, our porters hiked ahead of us to set up camp before our arrival. They set up their tents off to the side and were very private. I wanted to finish a conversation with one of our porters, so I approached their quarters. I noticed the porter setting up his own sleeping bag. It was a child's sleeping bag with Disney's Aladdin on it. That night we thought about how he slept in this bag, designed for a child to sleep on their floor, while we slept a few feet away in our mountaineering-grade bags. That stark contrast has never been lost on us.

In Western cultures, saving is often equated with sacrifice. Stepping outside of your normal environment can help illuminate everything you already have. People around the world who may look, act, and think much differently than we do have the same fundamental wants and needs. Gaining this understanding and overcoming fear enables us to pull yet another lever that is available to those who *Choose FI*.

GEOARBITRAGE

Tim Ferriss popularized the term "geoarbitrage" in his best-selling book *The 4- Hour Workweek*. Geoarbitrage is the act of exploiting differences in the cost of living between two locations. This allows you to leverage this difference by earning money in one area, then spend it in another community where those dollars go further.

Geoarbitrage can allow a life of great adventure for those who have achieved financial freedom. This enables them to work anywhere—or not work at all. Early retiree Jeremy, who writes *Go Curry Cracker*, and his wife Winnie, decided to employ geoarbitrage to enable them both to retire in their thirties. Jeremy said, "The idea was the first several years, we would go to extremely low cost of living countries. Even though we were living like kings of yesteryear . . . it just didn't cost very much." While living in Mexico, Central America, and Southeast Asia, "we were spending (about) two grand a month." They next decided to spend time living in Europe and reported spending three times as much—$6,000 a month—for the same lifestyle.

Bryce and Kristy, shared a similar experience. They retired in their thirties to pursue world travel. They tracked their spending, which totaled $40,000 in their year traveling the world. Spending $40,000 traveling may seem ridiculous and unachievable to some, but Kristy noted these costs represented their *total spending* for the year, compared to the $60,000 to $80,000 it would cost them to live a lesser lifestyle in their hometown of Toronto. In their first year traveling, they split time between Southeast Asia and western Europe, including a prolonged stint in the London suburbs, an area not known for a low cost of living. Their spending also included frequent luxurious massages and going out for fresh seafood meals in Asia.

When they returned to Toronto, they observed their friends spend more to support their lives, which generally revolved around working to make mortgage and car payments. Bryce observed, "Their cost of living is multiple times what ours is, and they're staying in one place working every day. They don't even get to enjoy their houses because they're working so much. Meanwhile, our biggest decision is, 'hey do you want to go to Japan next year or do you want to go back to Europe?' That's literally the decision we're wrestling with right now. So it's a really different lifestyle." It's worth noting the $40,000 Bryce and Kristy spent in their first year traveling the world included some rookie mistakes. In their second year, they spent only $30,000.

The globe-trotting stories of *Go Curry Cracker* and *Millennial Revolution* are fascinating. Still, many don't desire a nomadic lifestyle and aren't willing to leave family and friends to live in Southeast Asia or Central America. So does this eliminate geoarbitrage for us? Not at all. A different application of geoarbitrage is a powerful and common tool for those who *Choose FI*.

DOMESTIC GEOARBITRAGE

It's easy to think of geoarbitrage as a crazy thing that "other people" do, requiring a move to a faraway country. But you could do it in your own country, state, or even your own city. Just as the cost of living varies from one part of the world to another, geoarbitrage can be utilized locally. This theme is heard repeatedly among those who *Choose FI*, often with dramatic results.

Scott Rieckens, creator of the documentary *Playing With FIRE*, lived in beautiful but expensive Coronado Beach near San Diego when he decided to get serious about pursuing FI. He realized geoarbitrage was the easiest first step for his family. They could move from one of the most expensive places in the country and save significantly. They were paying "an insane amount of money in rent," which they needed two incomes to cover. Of course, higher earners pay higher income taxes, too. Especially painful is the fact Californians pay high state income taxes in addition to federal. Finally, two working parents also meant paying a nanny. Scott explained, "half my day is spent working so I can have somebody else watch my child."

Rieckens realized they would have to move to a less expensive area if they wanted to save money, which meant nearly anywhere else in the country. Geoarbitrage provided Scott and his wife a path to achieving FI in five to seven years. Even if their projection was "wrong on a pretty decent scale," they could still be financially independent far faster than they previously imagined.

Geoarbitrage was the focus of the conversation when Mr. Groovy, the writer of *Freedom is Groovy*, was interviewed on the *ChooseFI* podcast. Mr. Groovy and his wife moved from high-cost Long Island, NY to Charlotte, NC. Their story was a stark example of what is possible with geoarbitrage. They decreased their cost of living from about $7,000/month on Long Island to less than $1,800/month in North Carolina. They used proceeds from the sale of their Long Island condo to purchase a home for cash in North Carolina, and they still had capital left to add to their investments. One big decision allowed this couple to shed a big mortgage, high property taxes, and other elevated expenses to achieve FI. And they didn't have to sacrifice lifestyle, trading a 600-square-foot one-bedroom condo on Long Island for a two-bedroom place in Charlotte. According to Mr. Groovy, "I gave up nothing. The weather is nicer. The core government services are just as good as Long Island. I do the same thing in North Carolina as I did on Long Island."

When my wife and I got married in late 2005 we realized we truly wanted something different, so we decided to leave our high cost of living area on Long Island, NY and move to Richmond, VA. Even though we were both CPAs and could "succeed" on Long Island using traditional measures, we always felt we'd have to give something up (e.g., saving for retirement, travel, Laura staying home with our future kids, etc.), and we weren't prepared to mortgage our future and our freedom. So we made the tough decision to leave our family and friends and move 400 miles south, where the housing prices were over 50 percent less than Long Island. That one decision catapulted us on the path to FI.

We've discussed using domestic geoarbitrage to decrease expenses if you are going from a high cost of living area to a lesser one. Your willingness to move can also be used to increase income if going to a place with better opportunities. Either can be powerful tools on their own, but what if you could utilize "dual geoarbitrage," impacting both the spending and earning sides of the equation simultaneously?

That's what *Physician on FIRE* did. He lives in a small Midwestern town and is well compensated, making greater-than-average income for his medical specialty. The combination of lower living costs and higher demand for a physician in a smaller town can mean tens of thousands of dollars difference in the bottom line every year. A physician in his setting can be a "big fish in a small pond" without feeling the pressure a physician might feel to keep up with other big city high earners. Compare that to being in a city where the cost of living is higher and more people are competing for the same jobs.

Most medical professionals can incorporate these ideas, as I did in my career as a physical therapist. "Dual geoarbitrage" can also be powerful in a world that offers a growing number of opportunities to work from remote locations. My wife incorporated this strategy, working for a consulting firm based outside Washington, DC, earning commensurate wages and living in an area where dollars stretch further. This strategy can also be powerful for online entrepreneurs.

There are many ways to use mobility and travel to accelerate your path to FI. Don't believe that travel is a luxury, preventing you from getting out there and seeing the world in unique ways. Being mobile is a powerful tool for those who *Choose FI*.

ACTION STEPS

1. **Have you mastered the basics of living within your means and using a credit card responsibly,** paying off your balance monthly without paying interest? Perhaps it's time to step up your game and learn about the use of credit card travel rewards. Visit ChooseFI.com/travel for a constantly updated list of the best travel reward cards.

2. **What was the last adventure you had that pushed you out of your comfort zone?** Start planning the next one now. Maybe it's a camping trip with the kids or a service mission with a church or charitable organization. It doesn't have to be expensive or far away.

3. **Consider why you live where you do.** Would moving to a different location allow you to earn more, spend less on housing, or provide better access to your most desired activities? Brainstorm other ways you could use geoarbitrage to live better now while accelerating your path to FI. You can think big—like moving to another part of the world—or small—like moving across town to be closer to work or to an area with lower property taxes. Break through limiting beliefs.

PART 3

EARN MORE

You have brains in your head.
You have feet in your shoes.
You can steer yourself any
direction you choose. You're on
your own. And you know what
you know. And YOU are the one
who'll decide where to go.

DR. SEUSS
OH, THE PLACES YOU'LL GO!

CHAPTER

8

HACK COLLEGE (OR JUST SKIP IT)

This book is not out to bash college. Brad, Jonathan, and I all have college degrees. For Brad and me, those degrees were instrumental in our paths to FI. But "hacking college" is a common pattern among the people profiled in this book. "Hacking college" means getting degrees that enable high-paying jobs while accruing little to no student debt. Alternatively, you can accumulate valuable skills without getting a college degree. While income is important, the ability to save a high percentage of that income because we're not handcuffed by high student loan payments is even more important.

Contrast that with Jonathan's story. He did not hack college. At age twenty-eight, he graduated with $168,000 in student loan debt. Despite his remarkable story of paying off this huge debt in only four years, he was thirty-two years old before he was able to get his net worth back to $0. Some in the FI community who have optimized college are approaching or even achieving FI in their early thirties. At least Jonathan came out on the other side with a pharmacy degree that gave him the ability to earn a six-figure income. This provided a large shovel to help fill the financial hole he dug for himself.

Many people find themselves crushed by student loan debt.

Often, they're stuck paying interest for loans they acquired before they were even old enough to buy a drink legally.

And many have degrees that don't even give them marketable skills. They end up having to take jobs unrelated to their field of study to start paying back the loans. This traps many people on the standard path.

THE COLLEGE DECISION TREE

Depending on where you are in your journey to FI, this may be the most important chapter in this book for you. Or it may be irrelevant.

If you've already made the college decision, are in a highly paid career you're satisfied with, have no college debt, and don't have kids to help navigate these decisions you can probably skip or skim this chapter. You've already won this part of the game.

If you've finished college and are in a rewarding career, but school loans are handicapping your ability to save toward a FI lifestyle, you'll need to determine the optimal strategy to handle your loans so you can move forward.

If you've gone to college and found you're not satisfied with your career choice, you may need to gain further training to switch careers. Others among you may have found FI early in life before making the college decision. Others still may be working toward FI while simultaneously planning for your children's education.

If you fit into these categories, you will have a different decision tree. You should question the assumption that college is right for everyone. If you want to be a doctor or medical professional, lawyer, engineer, or accountant, that answer is clearly yes. For others, like those looking to be entrepreneurs, computer coders, trade workers, or pursuing a career in the arts, the answer is far less clear.

If you decide college is the right choice, you will need to determine how to get the most value while spending the least amount of time and money to get on the path to FI. We'll explore ideas, strategies, and stories from those who have successfully "hacked college."

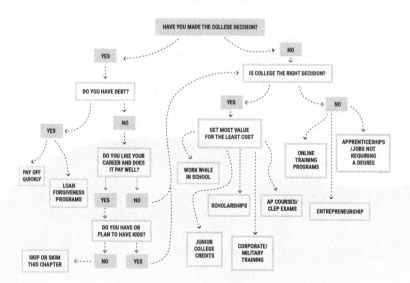

With two elementary school-aged daughters who are growing up fast, my wife and I are increasingly thinking about how to pay for college. We plan to challenge our girls to think differently and to challenge the status quo of going to the most prestigious college they're accepted to and paying the sticker price.

For example, the state of Virginia has a Community College "Guaranteed Admissions" program where if you attend a community college for two years, earn a certain GPA, and take specific courses, you are 100 percent guaranteed admission to prestigious state universities such as the University of Virginia and the College of William & Mary. So, you pay very little for your first two years of community college, the credits transfer and you walk out two years later with a degree from UVA or W&M!

If our girls really want to attend a university for four years, we'll task them with applying for private scholarships and merit scholarships— anything that makes them understand that paying for college is mostly going to be their responsibility and that the choice of where they attend can swing their net worth by potentially $200,000 over a four-year span.

BRAD

If college is not the right choice, you will still need to acquire the skills, knowledge, and experience that enables you to add value for others, enabling a well-paid career. We'll explore exciting alternatives that can set you on the path to FI without spending time and money for a college degree.

Choosing FI requires starting where you are and determining the right path for you. The remainder of this chapter will help you find the right path to follow on your journey.

DEALING WITH STUDENT LOANS

In an ideal world, this message would reach people as young as high school or earlier and change how we look at school, debt, work, saving, and investing. This would enable more people to get on the path to FI early. Unfortunately, the reality for many people looking to *Choose FI* is that they can't develop a high savings rate because they are hampered by student loan debt.

When I am asked about my biggest financial mistake, the answer is obvious: Going to pharmacy school. It took 12 years of my life and left me with $168,000 of student loan debt. I got back to broke at the age of thirty-two. This was only possible, however, because I focused my energy on paying off my debt with extreme intensity, at the expense of other goals.

Going to pharmacy school was a financial mistake, but it wasn't a life mistake. It's become part of my story and motivation to help people who are on a similar path. Your past doesn't define you. Many people find the concept of FI after having made significant financial mistakes. It's important to recognize past mistakes and address them. As the Chinese proverb says, "The best time to plant a tree was twenty years ago. The second-best time is right now."

If you're in that situation, it's important to determine the optimal strategy to pay the least amount of money to satisfy your financial obligations. That's not easy. There are multiple loan forgiveness programs with complex rules and conditions. Many people don't even know these programs exist, and there is no guarantee the programs won't change. Some companies look to capitalize on people's ignorance by offering a one-size-fits-all answer to refinance. While refinancing is good for some, it can cost others tens of thousands of dollars. Worse yet, once that decision is made, there is usually no turning back.

Travis Hornsby, founder of *Student Loan Planner*, spoke on the *ChooseFI* podcast about the options available to those burdened by student loans. Hornsby stated that his company saves their average client $60,000 because people make so many mistakes when paying back their student loans. The key point that Hornsby emphasizes is, "There's hope for people [with student loan debt]. That person can achieve FI, and maybe they didn't think they could before."

Hornsby shared two options for dealing with student loans. You can pay your loans off as quickly as possible, or you can seek loan forgiveness. Many of the rules he discussed are subject to legislative changes, and the information may be time sensitive, so we'll give a general overview. *Before implementing any strategy, do your own research to be sure that none of the rules have changed.*

The first strategy is simple and straightforward. Hornsby said if you owe less than double your salary and are employed by a for-profit company in the public sector, you should probably refinance. Get the lowest rate possible to reduce the interest. Pay the loans back as quickly as possible. Move forward with your life.

Hornsby emphasized that while refinancing to get a lower interest rate is the best option for many with student loans, you should be sure refinancing is optimal for you *before* making a binding decision. He said, "there's a lot of companies out there, and that's how they make their money. So they're prone to giving refinancing suggestions when maybe that's not the right path for you. And you have to be careful because once you refinance, all those other options are off the table."

If you have a greater than two-to-one debt-to-income ratio or if you work for a not-for-profit or government agency, a better option may be going for loan forgiveness. Hornsby broke loan forgiveness programs into two categories: the Public Service Loan Forgiveness (PSLF) program and the standard loan forgiveness program.

The PSLF program is the best option. To qualify, you must have direct federal loans. You also have to work for the government or an eligible not-for-profit organization. If you meet these requirements, you may qualify for an income-driven repayment program. You pay a percentage of your income (about 10 percent) for ten years (120 payments). At the end of that period, the remainder of your balance is forgiven without tax consequences. This can provide massive savings to those who qualify.

The second type is the standard loan forgiveness program, which is available to anyone. This program is also based on paying a percentage of whatever you earn, but you have to do it for twenty to twenty-five years instead of only ten years as with the PSLF. At the end of the standard loan forgiveness program, you also owe taxes on the forgiven balance. This makes the calculations for people considering this option more complicated. You have to figure out how much you would save by not paying back the full balance versus the need to carry a student loan balance for several decades and then pay the tax bomb awaiting you at the end of the program.

Loan forgiveness programs are subject to legal changes. Hornsby said he's discussed proposals to repeal and replace income-driven loan forgiveness programs with lawyers. They agree that the language of the loan agreements means people who already have outstanding debt have to be grandfathered in under existing rules. Hornsby also opined that the nation's current "$1.5 trillion of student debt is a massive problem. If they made the student loan system for current borrowers significantly less friendly, that would potentially create a financial crisis." While both are valid arguments for why these loan forgiveness programs are unlikely to go away or even change dramatically, it is important to acknowledge that there is no guarantee they will continue, adding an element of risk to these strategies.

While Hornsby offers options and hope to many who have already gone into debt, a more exciting conversation is available to those who have not gone down that road. There are many options to hack college or bypass it completely, gaining skills and knowledge to make more while spending less in the process of obtaining them.

IS COLLEGE THE BEST OPTION?

The first decision we have to make is whether college is the right decision. There are varying points of view on the value of college.

Some people point to outliers like Steve Jobs, Mark Zuckerberg, or Lebron James as examples of people who became tremendously financially successful without college degrees. With all due respect to everyone reading this, you probably don't have Jobs's creativity, Zuckerberg's network building acumen, or James's physical talents.

On the other side of this debate, people point to recent studies that show college graduates earn more to validate the importance of having that college degree. A study from Georgetown University found college graduates earn on average $1 million more than others over their lifetime. Another study by the Pew Research Center found college graduates earned about $17,500 more annually than high school graduates. These statistics make a strong argument for college.

Let's look at the pro-college arguments more closely. How many years would you have to work, earning an additional $17,500 annually, to reach the $1 million lifetime earnings advantage? Answer: more than fifty-seven years! If your goal is to lock yourself into a career, then work to earn as much money as possible over your lifetime, college probably does make sense. But what if you want to *Choose FI* and achieve it quickly?

Many people who purposefully pursue FI are able to do so in ten to twenty years. FI can be achieved in under a decade if you take a more aggressive approach. This requires adding variables to the equation to make an informed decision.

Don Wettrick is a high school teacher who is also the co-founder and CEO of StartEdUp Innovation program. He spoke about his program on the *ChooseFI* podcast. Wettrick challenges the conventional wisdom that everyone should go to college. He said, "You want to go to medical school? You got to go to college. You want to go into advanced engineering? Got to go to college." But what does he advise others, whose careers don't absolutely require a degree?

What if someone is considering a journalism degree? Wettrick said, "Start a freaking blog!"

College proponents argue there is more value to college than a degree, such as developing a network. Wettrick said, "You know who has an advantage? When you're [graduating college at] 22, you're everybody else." He points out that a sixteen-year-old who is genuinely interested and driven can start learning, creating, and gaining experience at a young age while everyone else is worried about grades and looking good on a college application. This can give that young person tremendous advantages.

Wettrick also points out that he's putting his money where his mouth is. He's letting his daughter, a high school senior, choose her own path in life. He said, "She's got a 3.9 [GPA], and at a minimum, next year, she's going to take a gap year. Minimum. She might not go to college." She wants to pursue the entrepreneur route.

Many career paths offer high-paying jobs that do not require a college degree. We'll consider some alternatives to college later in this chapter.

The next thing that must be considered is the opportunity cost of going to college. When you decide to invest your time and money in college, you are deciding not to invest those resources elsewhere. If your goal is to reach FI quickly, does it make sense to give up four, six, or maybe twelve years of your life going to school? Is it prudent to dig a hole of debt when you need even more resources to dig yourself out? It very well may be if college enables a career you'll love for the next thirty to forty years. But too often, people spend four or more years of their lives and tens of thousands of dollars and come out with no discernible skills that will enable them to get a job. Even if you do obtain the skills that enable career success, there is still another cost to consider.

That next consideration is sunk cost. Consider how hard it is to change course once you invest the resources necessary to start down a particular path. How many people really know what they want to do with the rest of their lives when they're eighteen years old?

I am a "success" story, achieving FI at the age of forty-one. I developed a specialized skill set as a physical therapist. The longer I continued my practice, the less sure I became that it was what I wanted to do for the rest of my life. But I felt trapped by my success. I spent seven years and tens of thousands of dollars getting degrees that enabled this secure, well-paying job. My parents also invested heavily in my education.

Disenchantment is common for many seemingly successful professionals who seek FI as a path to freedom from high-earning jobs that don't fulfill them. Barney, author of the blog *The Escape Artist*, described this scenario: "If you're middle class, if you've been to college, in some ways the problem that you have is you have that safe option. That removes your impetus, the pressure on you to be entrepreneurial. In some ways, early career success in a relatively safe occupation can be a trap, because what's happening is you are being acclimated to a regular monthly salary, which is incredibly comforting. That leads to a bunch of behaviors around not putting that at risk." This leads many to continue on well-paid but unfulfilling paths through life rather than pursuing the life they truly desire.

HACK COLLEGE

If you've made an informed decision that college is the best path for you, the next step is figuring out how to "hack college." This means extracting the maximum amount of value from your college experience at minimal costs, allowing you to graduate with a valuable degree and little or no debt. This doesn't require coming from a wealthy family that can write fat checks to send you to prestigious and expensive schools. But it doesn't happen by accident either, so let's explore how to hack college.

College is an investment. Rather than viewing college as a good decision at any price, look at the cost—both money and time—of obtaining a degree and the expected return from having that degree. There are many ways to hack college.

Sometimes, *Choosing FI* is as simple as looking through a different lens to see alternative solutions to a problem. As the saying goes, if you only have a hammer, everything starts to look like a nail. If you accept easy credit as a solution to your problems, it's easy to accumulate debt. However, if you remove that tool from your toolbox, you'll quickly discover other tools can get the job done.

The easiest thing you can do if you want to hack college is to forget everything you've heard about the importance of going to a prestigious (i.e., expensive) school. Robert Farrington, who writes *The College Investor* blog, shared his experience of working his way up the chain from part-time clerk to store manager at a Target retail store. Climbing the corporate ladder enabled him to earn $180,000 per year, which he described as average for someone in his position.

Farrington observed that having a degree is important in getting jobs and promotions in big companies, but often not for the reasons people think. When asked if he felt having a degree was a big piece of his career success, he replied, "Yes and no. It's one of those things that it's the paper that shows you care. Did it actually give me any skills to be successful? I don't think so."

While some companies have started to recognize that a degree is less of a necessity, others continue to use it as a screening tool. There is value in having a degree to check that box on the application, but it is wise to get the degree as quickly and as inexpensively as possible.

Farrington believes people are being oversold on the value of college based on what he hears from readers of *The College Investor*. People reach out to him after they've taken on too much debt to pay for degrees from prestigious universities. Some continue to accumulate debt pursuing master's or other advanced degree programs. He said, "the degree is only valuable for maybe the first eighteen months after you graduate . . . Employers want to know your experience and what value you bring to them. The biggest problem I see today is what I like to call the over-educated and under experienced . . . They end up still having to get the entry-level job that doesn't pay them enough to afford all that debt . . . They've really just dug themselves into a hole that put them ten years behind someone that didn't get over-educated and under experienced."

Farrington advises combining your education with your experience to maximize the value of your education and increase the return on investment of education spending. His advice leads perfectly into the next strategy employed by those who have successfully hacked college—working while going to school.

Most college students find it difficult to ignore people willing to throw money at them in the form of loans with no regard to how they'll ever repay them. I witnessed this repeatedly in my career as a physical therapist. Interns I mentored routinely had $150,000 to $200,000 debt by the time they finished school while preparing to enter an occupation with an average starting salary in the mid-$60,000 range. Several were advised not to work while in school so they could focus on their studies. This is great advice for universities that lose income if underperforming students have to drop out. But it's horrible, and sadly common, advice for the students who will be trapped with massive debt and facing decades of work to pay it off.

Farrington said he hired over one thousand people while working as a Target store manager. He said,

"The best hires were people that worked in high school and college and had that experience. Because college can give you some skills, but it doesn't teach you communication skills. It doesn't teach you on the job problem-solving skills. And in pretty much every single career, those are the two things that separate the successful from the not successful."

This statement resonated with me deeply. I worked throughout college in a variety of paid internships and jobs related to my field. This helped me to graduate college with no debt and two job offers. In contrast, many people I went to school with and students who I've mentored during my career routinely graduate with six-figure debt and no job prospects. They don't have a network and they lack experience, meaning they'll require extensive on-the-job training because they struggle with communication and problem-solving skills.

My wife had a similar experience to mine. She worked full-time and attended school full-time. She worked her way up from teller to assistant manager at a bank while graduating with honors with a B.S. in mathematics. While her degree allowed her to check that box and opened some doors when applying for jobs, her work experience and ability to manage the demands of school and work simultaneously are what employers focused on when interviewing her. She also had multiple job offers before graduation.

Cody Berman of *Fly to FI* was interviewed by Brad and Jonathan to provide an example of someone who had purposefully navigated college. He noted that working while going to school not only had obvious financial benefits, but work experiences should be chosen carefully to provide maximum value. He discussed a teaching assistant position he had while going to college that benefited him in multiple ways. He earned good money, and he could network with professors and other students, all while learning communication skills and becoming an expert at creating spreadsheets with Microsoft Excel. As an added bonus, the job also had a good bit of downtime for which he was paid to study.

In addition to the benefits Berman outlined, there are options like being an RA (Resident Assistant) in an on-campus dorm, allowing you to eliminate your housing costs. Other positions within a university can allow you to eliminate tuition. The take-home message is that working while going to school is one pillar to hacking college. By strategically seeking out work opportunities, you can get far more value than the dollar figure you see on a paycheck.

Before going to college, Berman also spent a lot of time researching another pillar of hacking college: scholarships. Many people don't bother trying for scholarships. They see it as an all-or-none proposition with little chance of getting their schooling paid for. So they don't bother trying.

Berman advises looking for scholarships offered through organizations within your community, specific schools you're interested in, or those associated with your nationality, your major, life circumstances, or interests unique to you. He then advises applying for as many scholarships as you're eligible for.

He makes a great point; developing a process of mass applying for many scholarships gives you pretty good odds of at least getting a few. These scholarships can be worth a couple hundred to a couple thousand dollars apiece. He said getting even a few small scholarships add up: "They go really far toward knocking out that student debt you don't have to pay down the road."

Berman streamlined the application process. He found applying for most scholarships required writing an essay. However, most revolved around the same five themes.

He invested time to write strong essays around each of these themes, then he applied for many scholarships, taking just a few minutes each time to fine tune the template essay, customizing it for the scholarship he was applying to.

5 COMMON SCHOLARSHIP
APPLICATION ESSAY THEMES

1. Why did you select your major?

2. What are your future goals?

3. What is your biggest failure and what did you learn from that experience?

4. Why do you deserve this scholarship?

5. What is your greatest accomplishment?

It paid off. Berman reports that he was able to obtain grants and scholarships totaling between $15,000 and $20,000 each year. Combined with other strategies, he reduced the $30,000 annual sticker price at his college to between $5,000 and $7,000 per year.

An interesting example of the niche scholarships Berman talked about was provided when Noah and Becky of the blog *Money Metagame* shared their story on the *ChooseFI* podcast. Both worked in high school as golf caddies. They learned of the Evans Scholarship, which was available to caddies who had good grades and demonstrated financial need. Both were able to take advantage of this program, and it paid their full tuition through college while they continued to add income caddying on summer break.

I received a similar niche scholarship that paid the majority of my tuition for graduate school. The scholarship was provided through the athletic department of my university for those who participated in the school's athletic programs. I never played a sport for the school. I did work, as required for my undergraduate degree in athletic training, with the university's athletes. This qualified me for this valuable scholarship worth tens of thousands of dollars that I would have never known I qualified for if I wasn't actively looking.

Travis Hornsby of *Student Loan Planner* never had student loans of his own. He only became interested in student loans when helping his then-fiancée deal with debt she incurred when going to dental school. When he was finishing high school, he looked for scholarships provided by schools looking to boost their academic profiles. He found scholarships offering full room and board to anyone who was a National Merit Semifinalist. He was able to find several of these types of scholarships at different schools, which he said "creates a bidding war" for those who know to look for them.

There are many interesting stories and opportunities for scholarships. But even if you can't get any, there are other options for others to pay for your schooling.

Robert Farrington said that working for Target allowed him to have some of his tuition reimbursed when going to school for his undergraduate and master's degrees. This is another common tactic among those who successfully hack college. The strategy is frequently utilized by those pursuing graduate degrees, looking to further education to increase income potential. People get advanced degrees at little to no cost using employer- or military-paid tuition programs.

I took this approach, as my employer paid for my Doctor of Physical Therapy degree in full. My wife also got two master's degrees—an MBA and a Master's of Operations Research—after she began her career. She paid only for her books while her employer paid tuition costs.

Another way to have someone else pay for your schooling is by performing military service. Gwen, of the blog *Fiery Millennials*, enrolled in an Air National Guard program that provided a full scholarship. She then obtained an academic scholarship that paid her entire college tuition. While many on the standard path believe it's impossible to go to college without rich parents or loans, Gwen was able to get two full rides to college. She wasn't able to "double dip," so she utilized the academic scholarship and graduated with no student debt plus credit for an additional eight semesters of college from the Air National Guard program if she chooses to go back to school in the future. Her work with the Guard contributed to her ability to save $10,000 by the time she graduated. This provided a solid financial foundation for her after college.

If you can't get some or all your college paid for, you can still lower the cost of a degree through intelligent planning and hard work. Both Cody Berman and Gwen each put tremendous thought and effort into strategically obtaining a college degree for minimal cost.

Each discussed slightly different strategies to earn college credits while in high school, including AP courses, CLEP exams, and dual enrollment with community colleges. These strategies have a double benefit. They enable you to obtain college credits at a far lower cost than if taking classes through a university. You can also shorten the time required to obtain your degree, decreasing the opportunity cost of time spent in college and out of the workforce.

Many of the people highlighted in this section incorporated more than one of the strategies outlined. This isn't an accident. It goes to show that for those willing to think differently, there are many ways to hack college. This allows you to get the value of a college degree at a fraction of the cost most think is required.

ALTERNATIVES TO COLLEGE

What if instead of locking into a specific path and committing the resources required to obtain a degree, you simply skip college? What if instead of becoming a white collar professional and putting your money into passive investments, you learn a trade to become a blue-collar professional? Then leverage your skill into a more active investment, such as a small business or real estate investments that have the potential for greater returns and more personal control over results? When you *Choose FI*, you're limited only by your imagination and willingness to create your own future.

If you've decided college isn't the right choice for you, you'll have to find another path to obtain the skills and knowledge that allow you to earn more. Becoming a skilled blue-collar worker is one option. Jobs like boilermakers, construction and building inspectors, electric power line installers, and elevator installation

and repair all offer median salaries greater than $50,000, and they have double-digit projected job growth. Other options for high-paying jobs without a degree include careers in public service, such as law enforcement and firefighting, real estate (agent, property manager) or sales. Many times, success in these careers will require an alternative to a traditional degree, such as getting a certification or working your way up from lower-level jobs with on-the-job training.

Alternatives to traditional four-year colleges have popped up, too. Examples include online computer coding programs that build on the idea that we need to learn a set of stackable skills.

In addition to saving money spent on a traditional degree, these programs offer the advantage of being able to change and adapt quickly. In a field like computer science that is rapidly evolving, skills learned at the beginning of a program may become outdated in the four years it takes to complete a traditional degree. You may also change your mind in that time.

Chad Carson shared an excellent example of what is possible if you choose a path that doesn't require extensive formal education. Carson attended Clemson University on an athletic scholarship, where he played on the football team as a linebacker. He graduated with a biology degree and began the process of applying to medical school, but he wasn't sure he wanted to take that path for his life. He realized that once he committed the time and resources to go to medical school, the next twenty to thirty years of his life would be predetermined—he would obtain his education and then work to pay for those years of training.

He opted to take a different path with less certainty but more options. Instead of devoting another four to eight years going to school to become a medical doctor, Carson elected to devote that time to educating himself to become an entrepreneur and real estate investor. The result? He achieved FI in his mid-thirties, approximately the same age as many physicians when they enter the workforce with hundreds of thousands of dollars of debt.

There is no simple answer for how to obtain the skills and knowledge that enable you to earn more. Whatever path you take, if you want to earn more you have to add value that others are willing to pay for. With effort, thought, and purpose, you can obtain valuable skills and knowledge without committing resources that trap yourself. This gives you the financial and personal freedom to have options in life as you *Choose FI*.

ACTION STEPS

1. **The action step for this chapter will be very specific to where you are on your path to FI.** Review the diagram with the decision tree at the beginning of the chapter to determine where you are on your journey. Then develop one to two specific actions to take the steps necessary to put yourself on the path to gaining the skills and knowledge that allows you to earn more without committing excessive amounts of time and money.

I can not do everything, but I can do something. I must not fail to do the something that I can do.

HELEN KELLER

CHAPTER

9

INVEST IN
YOUR CAREER

A low income can be a stumbling block for many looking to *Choose FI*. It's important to control spending, but there is a floor on how low spending can go. You can't squeeze blood from a stone. Let's review the savings rate equation:

$$Savings\ Rate = Savings/Earnings$$

Savings is simply the amount you earn minus the amount you spend or:

$$Savings = Earnings - Spending$$

The savings rate equation, stated a different way looks like this:

$$Savings\ Rate = (Earnings - Spending)/Earnings$$

Frugality can allow you to create margin quickly. Living on less has leverageable benefits, such as paying less tax and needing less insurance. Still, spending can only go so low before bottoming out.

Earning more is the other piece of the equation that allows you to increase your savings rate. While there is a floor on spending, there is no ceiling on how much you can earn.

HOW DO YOU ACTUALLY EARN MORE?

Many people get caught up in the limiting belief that it's hard, even impossible, to earn more. Don't you have to study for years to earn a degree to get a high-paying job? Don't you have to go into debt with school loans, small business loans, or mortgages to build a rental real estate portfolio? It is possible to use these strategies to increase your earning power, but they're not necessary. These thoughts start with a lack of understanding of how and why people make money.

Going to school and getting a degree is not a formula for making a lot of money.

A college degree allows some people to earn more because they have acquired skills that others value enough to pay for, such as engineers, those with tech skills, health care workers, and accountants. People in these professions are not highly paid because they have a piece of paper from a particular school. They are highly paid because they've acquired rare and specialized skills that people value enough to pay for. They add value to the lives of others.

Others acquire degrees from the same colleges. They have diplomas printed on the same paper. Yet they find themselves trapped in low-paying careers or working jobs unrelated to their field of study because the body of knowledge they developed is not highly valued by society.

Although I graduated with $168,000 in student loan debt, I chose a profession that paid a six-figure salary upon entry. That wasn't an accident. It was a choice based on the economics presented to me. In retrospect, there are much easier paths to a six-figure income than my chosen path.

I find the virtually unlimited amount of money that we let teenagers take out to get any degree imaginable maddening. Going $90,000 in debt for a job that pays $40,000 is financial suicide. The mantra of "every kid needs to go to college" seems shallow when compared to the decades of student loan debt repayment that are tied to this decision. The decision to go to college has to be viewed through a cost-benefit analysis because ultimately the student will be responsible for paying it back.

A similar situation can be found with entrepreneurs and real estate investors. Smart use of leverage in the form of debt can accelerate the growth and success of an entrepreneur or investor. But leverage is a double-edged sword that can amplify bad ideas and decisions, leading to disaster.

Successful entrepreneurs and investors aren't successful because they are daring risk-takers. They are successful because they first focus on adding value that others are willing to pay for. This was exhibited by Chad "Coach" Carson on the *ChooseFI* podcast.

Carson began his path to FI as a real estate investor and entrepreneur with no money or experience. This would stop most people dead in their tracks. But he had a desire to learn, a strong work ethic, and a lot of energy. As he described it, he was a "young pup" running around tripping on his ears. He just needed to find "old lions"—people with the money and experience he lacked—who no longer wanted to put in the time and effort he was willing to supply. He focused on how he could add value for them by putting in the work they didn't want to do, finding deals that they could share together with him. He obtained what he needed to get started as an investor and entrepreneur by providing value to others first.

Making more money is not rocket science. But it's not obvious either. Many people don't understand this most basic principle.

Adding value is the foundation on which this section about earning more is built. If you want to earn more, there are many ways to do it. But they all start with this concept. If you want to be valuable, you must add value to the lives of others.

YOUR CAREER AS AN INVESTMENT

We haven't gotten to the investing section of the book yet, so excuse me while I jump ahead for a minute. Investors talk about the compound growth of money. Three factors determine how much money you will accumulate.

1. The amount of money invested (principal);

2. The rate of return on investments; and

3. The time available for money to grow and compound.

This framework is frequently used to discuss investment portfolios of stocks, bonds, and real estate. But investments aren't limited to these asset classes. When starting your journey to FI, your biggest asset is human capital, not financial capital.

We define FI as the time when work becomes optional, but your ability to earn money by working is the engine that drives the train to this destination. Therefore, it's worth applying this idea of compound growth to your biggest initial investment: your career.

ESI Money is written anonymously by the former president of a $100 million corporation. *ESI* focuses on how to grow your career and maximize earning power. On the *ChooseFI* podcast, he introduced the idea that "your career is a multimillion-dollar asset." And he shared the math to prove his point. He calculated that someone with a starting salary of $35,000 per year, earning an average pay raise of 3 percent per year, and working for forty-five years will make $3.2 million over their working lifetime. Understanding the value of your career emphasizes the need to nurture, grow, and maximize its value.

Many people sleepwalk through life assuming they can just work hard and be treated fairly. Except it doesn't always work that way.

Even when it does, it can lock you into the typical lifetime of mandatory work so well known to those on the standard path through life. But focusing on growing your income by adding value to others *and* saving a large portion of that income gives you an opportunity to achieve FI quickly, making future work optional.

Career compounding is bound by the same variables that govern all investment growth. The goal for those *Choosing FI* is to shorten the number of years we have to work. So we *have* to focus on the other two variables.

1. How can you increase the principal (i.e., the amount earned)?

2. How can you increase the rate of return on your investment (i.e., the growth of your income)?

A common pattern among those who achieve FI quickly is to choose a career that commands an above-average income. It's popular to say you should "follow your passion." Others might say, "find a job you love, and you'll never work a day in your life." Those make great bumper stickers, but they don't typically work well in the real world. Maybe a better idea is to find a career that interests you and allows you to earn a solid income. Then learn to love it, or at least like it, while saving a high percentage of your income, allowing you to achieve FI quickly.

I often joke that I don't know how I ended up in the accounting field when I actively disliked it so much. All jokes aside, I feel my choice of accounting as a college major followed by my work with two international accounting firms and a Fortune 500-level private company gave me a solid taste of the working world and showed me exactly what I did and did not like about it.

More importantly, accounting is the language of business, and having that knowledge has helped my entrepreneurial career more than I could have imagined. Not only does it allow me to exert a level of control over our company finances that most company founders are unable to replicate, but also my accounting knowledge helped me look at the entire business model differently and directly led to my success.

Case in point: When I started with Richmond Savers, I realized the site would never have enough traffic to make money through the traditional affiliate marketing methodology (i.e., having a ton of site visitors and then earning a commission through them clicking on affiliate links).

What I did was put on my CPA's hat and look at the "Lifetime Value of Customer" and actually offered my "travel rewards coaching" service for FREE, knowing that those people would almost certainly use my affiliate links in the future. I was investing in my business and also looking at it as a hybrid online/real-world business instead of just as a typical blog.

It's unlikely that your passion at eighteen years old will be the same as your passion at twenty-eight, let alone sixty-eight. The beauty of achieving FI quickly is not that you get to retire and never work again. It's that after you achieve FI, you get to choose what you're passionate about and pursue it to whatever extent you want for as long as you want.

If you love what you're doing, you can keep doing it. This is more common than you may imagine for those who achieve FI. For example, Brandon, who blogs as *The Mad Fientist*, has one of the most popular blogs among the FIRE community. He writes about optimizing the path to FI so you can retire as soon as possible. Yet he found that while achieving FI quickly, he grew to enjoy his job writing computer code. He continued to work at it for a few more years until he was finally forced to quit when his company would no longer allow him to work remotely while he lived abroad.

If you find you don't love what you're doing, you have the freedom to change your mind. If you want to make more money, you're free to do so. If you want to pursue something that doesn't make any money, you can do that, too. The need to make money doesn't keep you trapped doing anything you don't want to be doing.

The choice of an initial career that commands a high salary gives greater ability to start saving and investing more quickly. Whatever career or job you choose, it's important to negotiate the highest starting salary possible. When you get pay raises, they are usually based on a percentage of your salary, so you want this starting number to be as high as it can possibly be. Educate yourself by researching what comparable jobs pay in your area. Document the value you bring to a company. Don't just focus on listing credentials on your resume or in your interview. Have concrete examples of how you can add value by improving the company's bottom line by helping them cut spending or increase earnings. You can also leverage a competitive offer at any point and be ready to take that offer if your employer doesn't counter.

Let's return to ESI's example of a $35,000 starting salary producing $3.2 million income with 3 percent raises over forty-five years. If that person started at $40,000, they would earn an extra half million dollars over their lifetime. Increasing the starting salary to $50,000, the lifetime earnings jump by an additional $1.4 million. While those numbers are jaw-dropping, they only change the starting salary and assume you grow your income by 3 percent each year. What if you focus on growing your income much faster as well?

If you're already in a career that you don't love, but it pays enough to give you the option of *Choosing FI*, it may be in your best interest to stay in that job and focus on growing your income. Let's return to ESI's example. We've demonstrated the effects of increasing the starting income. What if we look at what happens if you focus on accelerating the growth of the income you already have? Again, assume a starting salary of $35,000. Lifetime earnings jump by $1 million if you earn 4 percent annual pay increases instead of 3 percent. If you increase annual raises to 5 percent per year, you earn an extra $2.3 million over your career! It's a fun exercise, but we can't magically get a 5 percent raise instead of a 3 percent raise every year. That's the bad news.

The good news? You also aren't limited to growing your income by only 3 to 5 percent each year. With effort and planning, it's possible to increase your income more than that. Even better, you do have some control over how much you can earn. But you won't make more magically. You need to manage your career. That process can be further subdivided, learning to manage yourself and manage your boss.

MANAGE YOURSELF

Working hard is great, but you also need to work smart. Most people work hard. This keeps you employed. If you're lucky, you'll get the 3 percent annual raise. If you're really lucky to be in a thriving company and industry, you may get 5 percent. But do you want to rely on luck?

There are things you can do to increase your value to others. This is the most reliable way to increase your income. ESI pointed out that most people will do what is expected of them, but only a few exceptional employees are proactive in looking to increase their value. If you're not sure what you can do to be more valuable to your employer, just ask them. ESI noted that, in his experience as the president of a company, these conversations were rare, and he cherished people coming to him. If your boss would not want you to ask, it may be a sign it's time to find a new boss.

One thing you can do to increase your value is furthering your education. This builds on previous ideas of hacking college, becoming a lifelong learner, and incrementally making progress by obtaining skills that complement one another. ESI started with a salary of $40,000, earned an MBA paid for by his employer, and doubled his salary in only two years. If you rely on the 3 percent raise, you can double your salary as well . . . in 24 years! Many people in the FI community have used similar strategies. They utilize employer programs to get advanced degrees and training for free or at minimal cost, which they then leverage into higher pay.

I witnessed this in my own home when my wife earned an MBA and a Master's of Operations Research, both of which were paid for by a former employer while she paid only for books. Earlier in this book, we discussed the talent stack as a way of creating unique value. We live in a world where people frequently have a hard time finding a job. Those who do often complain of greedy corporations that only care about profit. My wife's technical skills and business acumen allowed her to obtain a job she loves with working conditions so good she changed her mind on the "retire early" part of FIRE. How did she find this job? She didn't. They found and recruited her. If you think this was luck, she got her last three jobs without having to apply for them.

Continuing your education doesn't have to be limited to formal degrees. Could you get a certification related to your particular field? Or how about developing skills and interests unrelated to your job to solve a problem for your company. An example from my own life was learning about investing while working as a physical therapist. As I learned, I realized the options in my company's 401(k) plan were less than stellar. Most small business owners are not well versed in personal investing, let alone choosing a plan suited for their employees. They offer a 401(k) plan because everyone else does, and many accept the plan they're sold with little understanding of the options. I approached my boss and explained our plan's high fees. I didn't approach him from the perspective of a disgruntled employee coming into his office to complain, but as someone who was willing to take the bull by the horns to help him improve the plan. This would save him, me, and everyone else in the company money while improving investment options. He agreed, and we improved the plan substantially. My boss saved money while also gaining the ability to offer an improved benefit to all employees, including me. I spent next to nothing educating myself on investing.

Do you think that adds value to a company? Could you do something similar to help your company?

If you want to be paid more, make yourself more valuable. You need to be proactive, seek ways to add value and develop a skill set. But sometimes that's still not enough. ESI emphasized that while you need to start by focusing on the things you can control, you should expand your sphere of influence to areas that others think they can't control. You not only need to manage your career, you have to learn to manage your boss.

MANAGE YOUR BOSS

The phrase "manage your boss" sounds a bit manipulative and nefarious. But ESI's advice came from a person who was "the boss." He's managed hundreds of employees in his career, loved employees who did this, and recommends you utilize this technique to grow your income.

Those who do more than expected and add value tend to reap the rewards with larger raises, bigger bonuses, and faster career growth. But it's not enough to just work harder. You need to understand what work is valued by those who control the purse strings. You also need to be sure your work is recognized by those people.

The first step to managing your boss is to be sure you understand what is expected of you. As you get clarity, make a list of the items that are most important in ways that are specific and quantifiable. This will eliminate any gray area and establish clear goals for you to work toward that will benefit your employer. Staying with our theme, you are clarifying how you will add value to your company.

Once you understand the expectations, you can exceed those expectations. Focus on over-delivering in the areas your employer most values. If the goal is to grow sales 3 percent, look for ways to grow them by 5 percent. If your goal is to reduce spending by 10 percent, find ways to reduce spending by 20 percent. If the goal is to hit a benchmark in six months, find a way to get there in five months. If you can do this, you will demonstrate value and the reasons you deserve to be paid more.

Doing better work is not enough to guarantee you'll be rewarded. As you hit and exceed these specific and quantifiable goals, keep your boss in the know. This can feel like bragging or taking too much credit, but remember, each time you do, it is an advertisement for you. You are your own personal brand, either becoming more valuable or losing value depending on how you are perceived. It's important to reinforce that you're hitting the goals and benchmarks your employer established. This reminds them you're a good employee who they will want to keep happy. It will also keep them informed that work is getting done so they can focus attention on other areas that further increase productivity.

This should work with any employer. If it doesn't, you have objective evidence of your value that distinguishes you when you are ready to move on to another position or employer that will value these efforts.

The personal capital you will use to develop a career and earn income is your biggest initial investment. Unlike most investments, there is no risk and no downside associated with the concept of growing your income. Most investments involve putting financial capital at risk in hopes of gaining a return. The process of investing in your career and developing personal capital will improve your life while serving others.

Staying on the concept of your career as an investment, remember there are three factors in the compounding equation: principal, rate of return, and number of years.

If you focus on finding a career with high earning power and invest in growing that career, you can get to FI faster.

ACTION STEPS

1. **Write down five problems or annoyances in your everyday life.** Do other people have these same problems? What product or service could you develop that would add value to others by addressing these issues?

2. **Meet with your boss** to establish clear expectations and goals for your position.

3. **Identify one skill you could obtain in the next year that would increase your value to your employer by at least 10 percent.** Start developing it.

4. **Develop a specific routine to keep your employer informed of your achievements** (e.g., weekly or monthly e-mail, a quarterly meeting, etc.) and put it on your calendar today.

5. **Consider other negotiating points if your employer can't pay you more or if making more money isn't your primary need.** Will your employer pay for your cell phone or car? Can you negotiate the ability to work from home or work flexible hours?

I can do things you
cannot. You can
do things I cannot.
Together we can
do great things.

MOTHER TERESA

CHAPTER

10

BUILD A NETWORK

t's not *what* you know, it's *who* you know. This cliché is widely known and accepted because it contains a lot of truth. Dan Miller, author of *48 Days to the Work You Love*, writes, "78% of jobs are never advertised anywhere." Worse yet, many advertised jobs are already filled by the time the advertisements are made public. If you are not well connected, there are two things you can do with this information.

One is to feel defeated and hopeless. This provides a great excuse for why you can't get ahead, get a good job, and make more money. It provides a reason to accept your position in life and affirm why you can't *Choose FI*.

The better option is to start building a network of people you want and need to know to get ahead. How can you build a network of those people? What will it take to get on the inside when one of those opportunities arise? Who has done or is doing what you want to do? What can you learn from them? This is part of developing the growth mindset that enables FI.

It's easy to say you need to connect with the right people. But how do you actually do it? Why would someone with the money, power, and influence you need care about you? If you're only worried about yourself and how people can help you, they probably won't.

Kristy of *Millennial Revolution* had an interesting idea. During her interview on the *ChooseFI* podcast, she said, "I think in the FI community, it's so easy for us to get along with each other because we really don't want anything from each other. You really know that people are just there to be authentic and to have your best interests at heart rather than just pushing things at you because they need a condition." This has been my experience in the FI community as well, but it misses a bigger point.

We can all take that approach to relationships. You don't have to be FI to be genuine, authentic, and caring. In fact, this may be a chicken-and-egg argument. Maybe being genuine, authentic, and caring sets people up for career success that enables FI because they add value to others. These traits also lead people to spend money in ways that enable FI, rather than being trapped in the cycle of spending every dollar they have trying to impress and outdo others.

Many people never get it. "Networking" has a negative connotation for many people. Some think it means nothing more than handing out business cards, sending out resumes, and overpromising while under delivering. Networking done right is all about building real relationships.

Understanding the Golden Rule —treat others the way you want to be treated—

is the key to building any relationship. Every major religion has its own version. This has been adapted in many ways over the years. Jordan Harbinger of the podcast *The Jordan Harbinger Show* puts a modern spin on this idea, coining the phrase "ABG"—always be giving. It serves as a corollary to the ABC acronym—always be closing—popular among salespeople.

The Golden Rule emphasizes a moral commitment to having the best interests of the other party at heart with no expectation of reciprocity. Living this way means helping those who need help by planting seeds of positivity everywhere you go. Ironically, the more you give without expectation of return, the more inevitable it becomes that you will find an army of people looking to help you.

Brad's backstory leading up to *ChooseFI* is a perfect example. When he began teaching others how to redeem credit card reward points for free travel, he didn't have a good model on which to scale his business. So he would schedule two thirty-minute calls and explain the process to people over his lunch hour while he worked as an accountant full-time. He didn't charge for his time. It was an inefficient way to build a business and a horrible way to grow his income quickly, but he was building trust and growing a network of personal relationships. He said, "my entire success with my three different websites, and certainly, my two most recent ones, *Travel Miles 101* and *ChooseFI*, comes down to those relationships."

You shouldn't help people with the expectation that they owe you something in return. But when you help people, more often than not they will want to help you, too. It's just the way the world works.

Only in the last two years have I begun to appreciate the power of "networking." Historically, I always attached a negative connotation to that word—it felt spammy or insincere.

In reality, "networking" means going through life with a generous spirit, meeting people with similar mindsets, and looking for ways to help. Inevitably, as you cultivate these relationships, good things happen, and opportunities open in ways that you can't anticipate.

*Networking can be done in many ways. Some of my most effective networking efforts have started in private niche groups online, cemented by meetups in real life. Seeing how powerful this networking effect has been for me led to the idea of trying to foster that environment for others. It led us to start local **ChooseFI** groups all around the world for people interested in pursuing FI. At last count, that has led to over 200 local groups in over twenty countries.*

JONATHAN

FINDING MENTORS

As you go about building your network, you will benefit by connecting with a variety of people. Former US Navy SEAL officer Chris Fussell discussed this concept on the *Tim Ferriss Show* podcast. He said, "you should have a running list of three people that you're always watching: someone senior to you that you want to emulate, a peer who you think is better at the job than you are and who you respect, and someone subordinate who's doing the job you did . . . better than you did it."

A mentor is valuable because they've already been where you want to go. They can take you under their wing, share past experience, and guide you. The alternative is to learn everything by trial and error. Unfortunately, finding a good mentor who has an interest in helping, teaching, and guiding you on your journey is usually not easy. So what can you do?

Let's return to the example of Brad and Jonathan building their relationship before launching *ChooseFI*. Jonathan had no experience with blogging or podcasting before they started the podcast. He valued Brad as a mentor, so he focused on adding value for Brad when he pitched him on partnering to start *ChooseFI*. Here's how he described his thought process in a conversation on the podcast: "You can't go to that person that has it completely all figured out. They've got a complete business model that's running. They don't need you or have time for you. There was room in Brad's life for someone to help introduce a new project and take it to the next level. He wasn't at the finish line yet. He was really close, but he wasn't at the finish line yet. I had to bring something to the table, so I brought an idea and I brought sweat equity."

*When Jonathan first pitched me on the idea to start the **ChooseFI** podcast, I was instantly drawn in by his excitement for the project and the lack of competition that existed at the time. But mostly I had a gut feeling that this was something I would love to be a part of. I have always felt a calling to spread the message of FI, but I didn't have an outlet for it. Sure, I was helping people save money using travel reward points, and that was fulfilling to a point, but I realized there was so much more I could do. I knew this was well worth the minimal risk.*

The great part about starting a website or a podcast is that there's a minimal cost, and I knew if it didn't work, it would have just been our own time that we "wasted."

There is no escaping the importance and necessity of adding value to others if you want to learn and earn more. Whether you are looking for ways to directly increase your income or to connect with others who can help you, the answer is simple: add value for others first.

GET REAL

Technology is a great way to connect with people. Social media sites like LinkedIn, Facebook, and Twitter create opportunities to connect with many people quickly. Spending a few minutes to connect with just a few people every day allows you to build a network of hundreds, even thousands, of contacts throughout one year.

While technology allows you to make many connections, it can contribute to unnecessary distraction that plagues many people. It's easy to accumulate hundreds of "friends" on a social network. Remember that it's far more important to develop real relationships with people you can help and who can help you.

As our digital world expands, personal relationships have become rarer and more valuable. It often requires more time and more money to develop personal relationships. *Choosing FI* involves frugality, but more importantly, it's about being intentional, spending our time and money in alignment with our values. It's important not to be penny wise and pound foolish. Going out to lunch with coworkers is a simple example. It's easy to calculate the cost savings of not going out to lunch, but it's harder to calculate the cost when you don't allow yourself these social opportunities. You can be smart about this. Building a network is not an excuse to mindlessly drop hundreds of dollars a month on unhealthy fast food while sitting around complaining about office politics. It means strategically spending time and money to develop meaningful connections with people who can positively influence your life.

Author and speaker Brian Tracy advises everyone to "invest 3% of your income in yourself to guarantee your future." As a valuist, I hate arbitrary rules about spending, but I love the underlying principle of investing in yourself. I suggest putting part of that investment toward building your social network. There are many ways you can do this, ranging from small things like going out to lunch with coworkers, to larger expenses, like going to a conference instead of opting for online tools to learn new skills. This is a small amount to invest with massive upside potential if you develop real relationships that can transform your life.

Scott Trench, author of the book *Set for Life* and cohost of the podcast *BiggerPockets Money*, shared a great example of this principle in action when he talked with Brad and Jonathan on the *ChooseFI* podcast. Scott shared the story of how he was invited to sit in on the meetings of a mastermind group of real estate investors when he was in his early twenties. He'd been invited by an older gentleman who he met through a chance conversation while sitting and talking on a park bench. He recognized the value in having access to these successful people, and he refused to let the opportunity pass him by. He approached each of them individually and offered to buy them lunch, hoping to have the opportunity to learn more from each of them. These meetings helped form the foundation that gave him the skills and confidence to become a successful real estate investor. His actions also led to a serendipitous meeting with Josh Dorkin, one of the founders of the real estate investing education platform BiggerPockets, who happened to share a coworking space with one of the people from the mastermind group. This led to Scott eventually taking a position with BiggerPockets, for which he later became CEO.

Scott could have saved a couple of bucks on those lunches if he wanted to be more frugal, but it's hard to argue against buying a couple of lunches when they turned out to be a pretty wise investment. The combination of building a real estate portfolio and his rapid career growth at BiggerPockets put Scott well down the path to FI by his late twenties.

ACTION STEPS

1. **Write down three social groups** you are already part of and do one thing this week to add value to each.

2. **Identify one person in your field or a field you would like to enter who you admire,** don't know, and would like to connect with. Make a list of five potential ways you can add value to this person's life, then make the connection.

3. **Which two or three stories in this book do you most relate to?** If you haven't already, find those people and connect with them through their websites or social media. Introduce yourself and start a relationship.

4. **Calculate 3 percent of your gross income.** Develop a plan to invest that amount to build your knowledge, skills, and social network in the next twelve months.

PART 4

INVEST BETTER

An investment in knowledge pays the best interest.

BENJAMIN FRANKLIN

CHAPTER

11

LAY A FOUNDATION UNDER YOUR INVESTMENTS

Developing a philosophy and plan for investing is important for those who *Choose FI*. That's why we've devoted a whole section of the book to smart investing. It's not an accident that the "Invest Better" section is this far back in the book after "Spend Less" and "Earn More." Your savings rate, the difference between what you make and what you spend, is the engine that creates investable wealth, which then creates ongoing income that enables FI. If you have no wealth to grow and maintain, all the investing knowledge in the world won't make a difference.

I didn't understand this when starting on my path to FI. I believed you became wealthy by investing. The limiting belief that investing was a complex process better left to professionals was deeply ingrained. I was convinced there was no way I could do this myself.

My parents introduced my wife and I to their financial advisor. Based on this referral, we trusted the advisor blindly. We had a substantial amount to invest due to our high savings rate.

We later learned we paid approximately eight times more in hidden fees than we thought we were, costing us thousands of dollars each year. Following horrible advice led to costly tax planning blunders that cost thousands more. This combination of excessive hidden fees and unnecessary taxes cost us nearly $20,000 in just one year. But we weren't ignorant just once. We willingly followed this advice for nearly a decade before taking the time to educate ourselves. Blindly trusting an advisor with our money was easily a million-dollar mistake.

The magnitude of our mistakes was extraordinary because our high savings rate enabled us to invest so much money so quickly. But many people share the same misconceptions that set us up for these mistakes. It's common to think investing is confusing, overwhelming, and impossible to do on your own. This is not an accident. There is a tremendous incentive for the financial industry to promote feelings of inadequacy, fear, and confusion in investors. Creating complexity and anxiety allows the financial advice industry to justify their existence. None of this creates value. Instead, it promotes complicated investment portfolios, high advisory fees, and excessive trading that benefits the financial services industry.

To be a successful investor, you have to build a strong foundation. This starts by understanding your investment strategy. You need first to understand the basic math that governs all investments. Then you must choose an investment path that both matches your individual strengths and abilities and gives you a reasonable chance to achieve your financial goals.

THE INVESTMENT EQUATION

Those on the standard path through life are typically advised to save 10 to 20 percent of their income into their 401(k) or other retirement accounts. If you start early enough, choose a great advisor, and the stars align just right, you should reach FI and retire securely, maybe even a few years early. If we return to the relevant portion of the chart from Chapter 4, adapted from the popular *Mr. Money Mustache* (MMM) article "The Shockingly Simple Math Behind Early Retirement," you'll see this sets you up for a standard forty- to fifty-year career.

Savings Rate (Percent)	Years Until Financial Independence
10	51
15	43
20	37

Unfortunately, most people don't save that much, meaning they may never achieve FI.

Let's review the three factors that govern investments and determine how much wealth we will ultimately build. Those factors are:

1. Amount of money invested (principal);
2. The rate of return on investments; and
3. Time available for money to grow and compound.

If you start saving and investing as soon as you start your career and follow the standard advice, you *should* reach FI in forty or fifty years. But this standard approach won't work if you want to achieve FI sooner. It also won't work if you are already in your forties or fifties and just starting to invest. In either case, time is not working in your favor.

If you're looking to achieve FI quickly, you will have to either increase the amount you invest, earn a higher rate of return on your investments, or do both simultaneously. The next few chapters dive into the specifics of three different strategies—investing in index funds, your own business, and real estate—that enable you to achieve FI quickly. This overview highlights the advantages and drawbacks of each approach.

THE SIMPLE PATH

The phrase "the simple path" is taken from the title of JL Collins's book *The Simple Path to Wealth*. This approach utilizes traditional paper investments (stocks and bonds) held in low-cost passive index funds. The simple path is consistent with solid investing advice from outside the FI world but with one big exception. Instead of saving 10 to 20 percent of your income as typically recommended, you combine strategies from earlier sections of the book to develop a higher savings rate of 30 percent, 50 percent, even 80+ percent for some. The higher the savings rate, the shorter the time to FI.

Several aspects make this approach appealing. It works well for those who can develop a high savings rate because they earn a high income, live frugally, or some combination of the two. It is simple because it requires little effort after you learn what investments to put your money into, set appropriate expectations, and learn to manage behavior.

Following this path simply requires going to work, getting a paycheck, and adding as much of that paycheck to your investments as often as possible. Wash, rinse, repeat, and FI will be inevitable. You largely control the time to reach FI by the size of your savings rate. This frees up time and energy to do what matters most to you rather than spending time month after month trying to determine how and where to invest.

I'm a CPA who theoretically should have some knowledge of financial statements, markets, etc., but I always felt a level of anxiety trying to understand the stock market. It just always seemed like gambling to me or something that could only be navigated with the help of an "expert."

*Then I found John Bogle's book **The Little Book of Common Sense Investing** and JL Collins's **The Simple Path to Wealth**, and I finally understood that essentially nobody could outperform the market over a forty-year timespan. Furthermore, and perhaps most crucially I learned that fees matter. In an ode to "control what you can control," what you can control with investing is cutting down your fees, both financial advisory fees and expense ratios on mutual funds.*

While these sound small at a mere 1 percent (insert sarcasm here), combined they can take away over half of your compounded potential net worth forty years down the road. That's insane!

Now I am content matching the market by buying low-cost total stock market index funds and focusing on pumping as much money into those funds as possible month after month, year after year with the full anticipation that I'll have performed better than any of those "experts" could have done when factoring in the corrosive impact of fees.

This path to FI has challenges. The first is that having a high savings rate is the only lever you can pull. For those with low incomes, student loans, or other personal challenges that prevent having a high savings rate, this path to FI is slow until you can address those issues.

Another challenge is the lack of control over investment performance. The beauty of the simple path lies in its passivity, but the flip side is that it requires you to accept the returns the market provides and trust that your assumptions based on the past will be true in the future. You are relying on markets to perform while you have no control over that performance. In a worst-case scenario, future returns may not match past returns. Even in a best-case scenario, it is unrealistic to assume returns will exceed the past. This means your upside is limited to 10 to 12 percent annualized average returns with a lot of variabilities.

Many people in the FI community love to talk about using high savings rates, index fund investing, and the 4% Rule as a pathway to a better life. You can get off the hamster wheel of spending thirty or forty years of trading time for money. For high earners, the simple path makes FI possible in a decade or less.

For others, the simple path can be defeating. Those with lower incomes, student loan debt, larger families, or other financial challenges hear about people saving 30 percent, 50 percent, even 80+ percent of their incomes and tune out quickly. It does no good to learn that a married couple can save over $50,000 per year in tax-advantaged retirement accounts when your household is only bringing in $40,000. Others have made mistakes in the stock market in the past and have no interest in jumping back in. Some on the standard path don't discover the concepts that enable FI until their forties, fifties or even sixties, but it can be more difficult to make the changes necessary to implement the concepts that late in the game.

Many people on the standard path through life are skeptical of the whole idea of FI. At best, FI is an interesting concept for the privileged. At worst, it's viewed as impossible. This may be true if you limit yourself to the simple path, but there is no reason to limit yourself.

THE ACTIVE PATH

The active path involves investing in building your own business. There is significant upside for those willing to take the active path. Rather than being passive and relying on financial markets, you have far greater control over your investment outcomes. There is no limit to the returns you can achieve. Instead of 10 percent annualized returns, you could grow your investment by ten times or more in a year with the right idea, effort, and timing. In fact, there is no ceiling when investing in your own business.

The active path also allows you to turn your sweat equity into money. Paper investments require starting with some financial capital, which then compounds over time. Investing in your own business allows you to create value with your ideas and effort. Your personal capital has the potential to grow at a more accelerated rate.

Investing in your own business allows you to add leverage to your returns. Many people associate leverage with debt and assume this path is risky. That doesn't need to be the case. There are many types of leverage. For example, you can develop a product ranging from writing a book to developing an app to designing a t-shirt, then sell the product at scale. You can leverage the efforts of multiple employees working for you. Leverage allows you to increase returns far beyond what is reasonable to expect with passive investments. Leverage used wisely allows you to accomplish this with little risk of losing money.

Investing in your own business also gives you access to tax advantages not available to those who earn income as employees. The benefits include the ability to access additional tax-deferred investment accounts, shift personal expenses paid with after-tax dollars to tax-deductible business expenses, and structure income to be taxed more favorably.

The active path has its downsides. You run the risk of the business failing along with the financial loss that goes with it. It is true that the wealthiest people in the world get there through investing in a personal business. It is equally true that many businesses fail before ever getting off the ground. The simple path allows you to collect a predictable paycheck and diversify your money across thousands of businesses with a strong track record. The active path can mean putting all your eggs in one basket with no guarantee of any income or growth.

THE HYBRID PATH

The third investment path commonly taken by those who *Choose FI* is real estate. Real estate is a hybrid of the other two paths.

Some aspects of real estate are similar to those of passive index investing. Stocks and bonds produce passive income in the form of dividends and interest. Real estate investing can produce regular income in the form of rent payments for landlords or interest payments for lenders. Each can be fairly passive income after applying the initial effort to select the right properties and people to work with. Stocks are investments in companies whose value tends to grow over time. Real estate values and rents tend to appreciate at, or slightly greater than, the rate of inflation. This provides passive growth of your investment. Like other passive investments, you must either have or borrow money to purchase these assets.

Real estate has many characteristics of a small business as well. It provides a tax shelter, allows you to incorporate leverage, and enables you to use your knowledge and sweat equity to amplify returns. You must do some upfront work to select a good property. You need to do the work yourself or hire and supervise others to maintain properties. Finding good tenants and screening out bad ones is also vital to your success. The number and quality of your investments and your management style and efficiency all factor into how much work is involved.

These factors allow real estate investors to achieve higher returns and more income than can be expected using passive investments. But remember, that's because they're not passive. Like other small businesses, they require more effort than a truly passive investment.

COMBINING STRATEGIES

It makes sense to focus on one strategy to avoid being overwhelmed when getting started, but it's important to understand you're not limited to just one strategy. There are many ways to combine investment strategies to accelerate the path to FI. These strategies can be used simultaneously, or you can switch from one strategy to another as it makes sense to you.

If you are just starting on the path to FI, you may benefit from house hacking, a concept introduced in Chapter 5. Remember, house hacking means buying a multi-unit house, living in one unit, and renting out the others. This allows you to reduce or eliminate your housing costs. If done well, you may even make a small profit. House hacking allows those with little or no money to obtain a real estate investment and have their shelter paid for by their tenants. At the same time, the money that you would otherwise pay for housing can be directed into index funds. This allows you to accelerate the path to FI by using both strategies in parallel.

You may already be on the path to FI with a high-paying career that enables maxing out all available tax-advantaged savings. You can direct other money into buying a property each year to start investing in real estate while providing an additional tax shelter. Another option is to start a side business while working a regular job, using sweat equity to produce an asset that can help you reach FI sooner.

Index investing is an incredibly powerful vehicle to reach FI. JL Collins rightfully calls it "the simple path." Save 50 percent of your income, invest in low-cost broad-based index funds for 10 to 15 years, and you're done!!

Building ChooseFI and meeting so many entrepreneurs over the past two years have really opened my eyes to the power of entrepreneurship and how it can give you some of the benefits of FI long before you reach your number. Though I haven't achieved FI, being my own boss means I have total control over my schedule.

JONATHAN

The concept of the "Red X Month," introduced on the podcast by Vincent Pugliese in episode 59, cemented this for me. If I wanted to take four weeks off for family reasons, I could put a red X through those dates on the calendar. Then I could work backward and build my schedule around that. I didn't need to go through a manager to see what's available after the senior employees choose their time off. I was working on the things I wanted to work on, and I felt like what I was working on had a greater purpose. Even more amazing was that my income had the potential to grow based directly on the work I put in. Instead of an annual 1 to 3 percent raise from my day job, we could grow the business week by week.

These tangible, measurable results essentially created equity out of thin air. And while the business didn't replace the income from my day job early on, I realized it had massive potential. I have a healthy respect for the power of entrepreneurship to speed up the path to FI and give you some of the benefits before you hit your number.

The awesome thing is you aren't limited to one path. Life is the ultimate choose-your-own-adventure story. I still invest in index funds, but I am using entrepreneurship to generate income to do that.

You can change investment strategies at any point along the path to FI, or pick multiple strategies. This is what I'm doing. My wife and I reached FI by utilizing the simple path. We started down this path because we didn't realize there were other options. By the time we learned about investing, we were established in our careers, developed a high savings rate, and had a young child. It made sense for us to continue directing our money into passive investments while using our free time to enjoy our lives. The downside of no longer trading my time for money now that I am "retired" is I don't have extra money to continue investing in passive investments. The upside is I have time to invest in creating new income streams. I'm doing this by building a web-based business. This book is also an asset that required little financial investment for a potential ongoing income stream. (Thanks if you bought it. Bonus frugal points for you if you got it from the library or a friend). I'm also considering diversifying some of my paper assets into real estate. This would earn higher anticipated returns, and I would continue to learn new skills, make social connections, and give myself continued purpose.

This chapter introduced the best investment options available to enable FI and demonstrated some ways to use them alone or in combination. Next, we'll explore each path in depth.

ACTION STEPS

1. **Determine which investment path matches your financial needs and lifestyle goals.** Pay particular attention to the upcoming section of the book to get ideas you can incorporate into your own investing plan.

2. **Review the full chart in Chapter 4 on page 67** connecting the savings rate to the number of years to achieve FI. Determine how many years it would take you to achieve FI using the simple path. Does this make sense? Or do you need to change investment approaches or add another approach?

Investing is not nearly as difficult as it looks. Successful investing involves doing a few things right and avoiding serious mistakes.

JOHN BOGLE

CHAPTER
12

INVEST IN INDEX FUNDS
AND UNDERSTAND
THE 4% RULE

Many people think investing is difficult. I certainly did, and it led me to follow bad advice and make expensive mistakes that lengthened my journey to FI. People assume being a good investor requires considerable skill and effort. You have to research the best stocks, bonds, ETFs, or mutual funds, then you have to know when to buy and when to sell them. If you don't know how, you have to find a smart, talented, highly educated advisor to hold your hand or do it for you. All of this is wrong!

If you select the simple path and choose to invest in index funds, you don't need to have specific skills or apply much ongoing effort. In fact, thinking you can improve investment results by developing your investment skill is likely to do you more harm than good. The key to success is living your life while allowing your investments to take care of themselves.

JL Collins's writing on investing has influenced many of us in the FI community. His book *The Simple Path to Wealth* grew out of a series of posts on his website jlcollinsnh.com, which began as a series of letters to his daughter he started writing after unsuccessfully trying to talk to her about money when she was home on a break from college. She interrupted the lecture and made the following statement: "I know this is important. I appreciate money. I know I need it. I just don't want to have to think about it and manage it."

As a young adult, investing always seemed out of reach. If I hadn't stumbled on JL Collins and his wonderful Stock Series, I likely would have ended up paying a percentage of my assets in advisory fees every year. It would have been a mistake that would have cost me hundreds of thousands, if not millions, of dollars over my investing career.

I realized index investing is doable. I don't need to beat the market, I just need to keep up with it. The fact that the best of the best active managers struggle to keep up with the market over extended periods cemented it for me.

Look at the trajectory of the market over any ten-, twenty-, or thirty-year period. The key is to participate and ignore the noise. I haven't looked back. When the market does well, I'm excited. When the market goes down, I view it like it's going on sale. Fear is no longer part of this equation.

JONATHAN

According to Collins, his writings gained popularity when he curated them as "The Stock Series" on his blog and then published them in *The Simple Path to Wealth*. He began to get more feedback from sophisticated investors. They thought his advice was great for others who, like his daughter, had little to no interest in investing and didn't want to put in the work. However, he points out, while this is typically meant as a compliment, it exposes a weakness many of us have. Collins practices what he preaches. He said,

"If I thought you could put in a little bit of work, or even a lot of work, and get better results than index investing . . . I would certainly be doing it."

A benefit of following a simple index investing philosophy is that it allows you to achieve outcomes greater than the vast majority of investors. The real power in following this philosophy is that you can obtain good results without taking away time or mental energy from other things that enable you to live the life you want. Combined with a high savings rate, the simple path provides an investment approach that enables you to achieve FI quickly.

One of Collins's controversial points is that "the market always goes up." Anyone who has ever watched the news or picked up a newspaper knows this is not true. On any given day of any week, the market can fluctuate up or down by a percent or two of its value—and sometimes much more. This is the equivalent of billions of dollars gained or lost. The worst single-day drop for the Dow Jones Industrial Average occurred on "Black Monday," October 19, 1987, when the market's value dropped by 22.6 percent. A graph of stock prices over a day, week, month, or even a year can look a lot like the printout from an EKG heart monitor, with peaks and valleys interspersed.

But if we zoom out and look at stock market performance over a longer period, say five years, the picture starts to look much different. Instead of seeing a bunch of seemingly random peaks and valleys, you see a smoother line trending in one direction. Zoom out to ten years, then twenty years, then fifty years, and the same stock price graph looks completely different. The line connecting these points smooths while traveling consistently up and to the right.

There is a clear trend that over time the stock market does indeed continue to rise. This isn't an accident. The stock chart in the short-term is a picture of investors' erratic behaviors, often driven by fear and greed. The long-term stock chart is a reflection of economic reality, driven by economic growth and inflation. When you invest in an index fund, you are buying shares in many companies that, in sum, are the economy. Individual companies can and will fail. The worst that can happen with any individual company is that they lose 100 percent of their value. At the same time, they are constantly being replaced by new companies that can grow by 100 percent, 500 percent, or even 3,000 percent. There is no cap on the upside.

Buying an index fund means making a bet that the system will continue to grow and prosper. Some will argue that this will not always be the case. After all, societies and economies have collapsed in the past. While this is true, I'm not basing my plan around a worst-case scenario that may never come.

If and when the day comes that we have a complete collapse of the economy with no recovery, our society will likely collapse with it. If this happens, will our government be able to honor bonds? Will your small business remain viable? Will real estate hold its value (and will private property be respected)? Most likely, our investment strategy will be the least of our worries in this worst-case scenario. If you base your plans around a "Black

Swan" event, you should probably invest in batteries, bottled water, and bullets.

THE FALLACY OF PICKING WINNERS

The next thought is if some companies go to zero while others grow exponentially, the key to investing must be to pick the best companies while avoiding the bad ones. There is only one problem with this approach: it doesn't work with any consistency or predictability.

Every year S&P Dow Jones releases the Standard and Poor's Indices Versus Active (SPIVA) report. This is a scorecard of stock indexes, collections of companies grouped together, versus actively managed mutual funds, which try to pick the best stocks from those indexes then buy and sell them in an attempt to beat the market. Year after year, results are predictably similar. Index funds outperform the vast majority of actively managed funds. Beating the market requires spending time and money on research. It also requires overcoming fees and taxes generated when buying and selling stocks.

Overwhelming evidence shows that few individuals, even professional fund managers, can consistently beat the market. Even if some can, it is impossible to know who they are in advance. Your best bet at investing success is to buy low-cost, passive index funds and to hold them forever to minimize trading fees, management fees, and taxes. When Vanguard founder John Bogle, who introduced index fund investing to the masses, talks about "doing a few things right," this is what he means.

Bogle sums up the fallacy that you can pick winning stocks succinctly in a quote from his book, *The Little Book of Common Sense Investing*: "Don't look for the needle in the haystack. Just buy the haystack!" Some argue that Bogle is biased in favor of index funds. Fair enough. So what did Warren Buffett, the most famous investor of this generation, who built a massive fortune picking stocks, write about index investing? Regarding managing his estate after he passes, Mr. Buffett wrote in his *2013 Annual Letter to Berkshire Hathaway Shareholders*, "My advice to the trustee couldn't be more simple: Put 10% of the cash in short-term government bonds and 90% in a very low-cost S&P 500 index fund. (I suggest Vanguard's.) I believe the trust's long-term results from this policy will be superior to those attained by most investors—whether pension funds, institutions or individuals—who employ high-fee managers." To be clear, Mr. Buffett suggests Vanguard; I don't disagree.

The other frequent mistake investors make is thinking they can time the market. If the market fluctuates up and down, doesn't it make sense to buy when the market is low and sell when the market is high? This allows you to get the upside of market gains while avoiding market losses. This would be a great idea if it worked. Unfortunately, there is no way to do it consistently.

We know the market fluctuates up and down. We know that over time, the market reflects the economics of the businesses it represents. But fear and greed drive the day-to-day volatility of the market. These behaviors can be irrational and unpredictable. That makes trying to time the market correctly futile. It is easy to predict that markets will go up and down. It is difficult to predict when and by how much. Doing it consistently is impossible.

Investors take different approaches to try to beat the market by stock picking and market timing. There are also plenty of people who go to Las Vegas and put their money into slot machines, on blackjack tables, or on red or black at the roulette wheel. Most gamblers make bets they *could* win, but, statistically, it's more likely they'll lose. Be an investor, not a gambler.

AVOID SERIOUS MISTAKES

Returning to the introductory quote for this chapter, John Bogle said investing is about doing a few things right and avoiding serious mistakes. Almost all serious mistakes investors make are a result of bad behavior. It's important to learn history, so you don't repeat those mistakes. The best way to avoid behavioral mistakes is to develop systems, remove yourself and your emotions, and allow the process to do the work for you. Part of the process of being a passive investor is acknowledging that the road is bumpy and you will be subject to some luck, accepting those facts and then proceeding anyway.

The best way to accomplish this is to focus on things you can control, particularly earning more and spending less to develop a higher savings rate. You will then add as much of your savings as often as possible to your investments. When the market goes up, your invested money will grow. When the market dips, new money you invest will go toward buying more shares. No matter what the market is doing, you'll be progressing toward FI.

Most investors fear market dips. It's painful to work hard for your money, save and invest it, then watch it drop in value. In reality, these drops are the best thing that can happen for those accumulating money while working toward FI. They allow you to purchase investments while they are "on sale" at discounted prices. When the market goes up—and remember, it always goes up over time—you will own more shares that have more room to grow.

The biggest mistake that investors make is getting it backward.

In life, people get excited by sales, which make them eager to buy. With the stock market, however, people become afraid and stop investing when things go on sale.

On the flip side, most of the time people get turned off and buy less when things get expensive in the retail world. With the stock market, many people get caught up in the hype of big stock market returns and actually buy more when the market is doing well. They buy stocks at exactly the wrong time after prices have already been run up. Fear and greed drive irrational behavior, making markets unpredictable in the short-term and market timing so difficult.

Controlling behavior is easier said than done. Avoiding destructive behavior is a difficult part of investing. Part of that is having a consistent plan in place to buy regularly, automating investment decisions whenever possible, then turning off your brain and getting out of the way. Another part is accepting the risk.

MANAGING RISK

There is always risk and reward when investing. You can take your money, put it in an FDIC-insured bank account, and be guaranteed you'll never lose a penny. Of course, this also guarantees your money will not grow and work for you. The price of everything—a loaf of bread, a car, college tuition—increases over time as a result of inflation. If your money isn't at least matching inflation, it's losing value. This requires you to take some risk to grow your investments.

At the same time, you don't want to risk more than necessary to accomplish your financial goals. When people talk about risk with paper investments, they're typically talking about volatility. Volatility is not the same as risk. Volatility can be used to your advantage when you are accumulating wealth that enables FI. It allows you to buy more shares at reduced prices. But volatility can introduce real risk.

The first real risk is when a person overestimates their ability to control their behavior during periods of volatility. When markets drop, it can be gut-wrenching to see your wealth cut by 10 percent, 20 percent, even 50 percent or more. Worse yet, you never know when you're at the bottom and how much lower it can go. Remember, you haven't lost anything yet—the market always goes up. But when you lose your nerve and sell, everything changes. People who sell in fear tend to remain fearful and don't get back into the market until it has gone back up. Some never get back in. This locks in real losses and is a real risk.

The second real risk is when you reach a point in time when you are FI and are ready to live off your portfolio. In this case, you have to sell off your investments to produce cash to support your lifestyle. If the market crashes, you'll have to sell more assets to produce the same amount of income, putting you at risk of running out of money before running out of life.

A big piece of managing risk is having an appropriate asset allocation. This can mean holding other asset classes, such as bonds. Stocks have higher returns, but also tend to have greater volatility. Bonds tend to have lower returns and less volatility. The key is to find the right mix to allow you to reach your goals without exposing yourself to excessive volatility risk that can cause you to sell at the wrong time, either out of panic or need.

CHOOSE FI

JL Collins's simple path consists of holding only one fund during your accumulation phase: a total stock market index fund that holds shares of every publicly traded US company. This will most likely give you a bumpy ride, with a lot of volatility. If history gives any indication of the future, this should reward you with handsome returns. Once you reach a point in life where you may need to live off your portfolio, Collins suggests adding a total bond market index fund. This will decrease volatility and smooth out the ride. You can choose if, when, and what amount of bonds to add to your portfolio to match your investments to your life stage, financial needs, and temperament.

People will argue whether you should have more diversification in your portfolio. These alternative portfolios start on the simpler end of the spectrum with "Lazy Portfolios" designed by the Bogleheads, fans and followers of John Bogle's index investing philosophy. An example is their popular Three-Fund Portfolio which adds a bit more diversity to a portfolio by including a total international stock index fund alongside domestic stock and bond funds. On the more complex end of the spectrum is investment educator Paul Merriman's "Ultimate Buy and Hold Portfolio," consisting of ten stock funds plus bonds. These portfolios add alternative asset classes, including international funds, real estate investment trusts (REITs), or tilt a portfolio to give more influence to smaller companies or companies that are perceived as undervalued.

This is where many people become confused and frustrated with the complexity of investing and get stuck with paralysis by analysis. It's wise to research different portfolios before getting started, but it's important to recognize that these strategies are more similar than they are different. Focus on getting the big things right. Low-cost, tax-efficient index funds should give you the best chance of success as an investor. It's impossible to know in advance what the optimal asset allocation will be going

235

forward. It's far more important to choose a portfolio that you understand and will stick with than to try to chase after the elusive "optimal" portfolio.

Earlier, we discussed buying low and selling high, but it's impossible to time markets with any consistency. One advantage of owning multiple asset classes is that it gives the option to rebalance periodically. The idea is to set a target allocation, say 80 percent stocks and 20 percent bonds. Then if one asset outperforms the other, you sell the asset that performed better to buy more of the asset that performed worse, bringing you back to your target allocation.

Rebalancing on a set schedule—say, once each year—forces the discipline of selling assets that are relatively high and using that money to buy assets that are relatively low. It provides a mechanical and unemotional way to control risk by taking some chips off the table. Selling assets that have performed better can help you improve investment returns by purchasing investments that have performed worse and are more likely to be better values. Rebalancing gives those who think they need to "do something" with investments something to do that may actually do more good than harm.

THE 4% RULE

The whole point of saving and investing your money is to build a portfolio that will provide the income you need to support your lifestyle, independent of the need to go out and earn money. So how do you know when you have enough? The FI community uses the 4% Rule as the starting point to answer that question.

The 4% Rule is based on historical stock and bond market data that suggests you can withdraw 4 percent of your portfolio the year you start retirement. You can continue to withdraw that same amount of money, adjusted annually for inflation, every year going forward with little chance of ever running out of money. So if we use the inverse of 4 percent, we would need to accumulate twenty-five times our annual expenses to be FI. For example, if you currently spend $40,000 per year and want to maintain that spending, you would need a portfolio of $1 million. *($1 million x 0.04 = $40,000)* If you spend $100,000, you would need $2.5 million. Conversely, if you spent only $30,000, you would need $750,000.

The 4% Rule is a great guide for those taking the "Simple Path" with our investments. While it gives us a starting point, it's not quite that simple.

You don't have to have a Ph.D. in finance to follow *The Simple Path to Wealth*, but it doesn't hurt to have one—or at least know someone in the FI community who does. Karsten Jeske—aka Big ERN—is that guy. He writes the blog *Early Retirement Now*. Jeske likes the concept of having a fixed round number that works all the time, but he's done the research and that number doesn't exist.

ERN uses this analogy to explain the concept. Figuring out how much money you need to be FI is like figuring out how long it takes you to drive from your house to the airport. The 4% Rule is like finding the average driving time to the airport by entering it into your GPS. It will give you a rough idea of how long the drive will take, but that time varies depending on the time of day and other variables. If you sent a driver on the same route every hour over a twenty-four hour period, some would leave at 3 a.m. with no traffic on the road and arrive at their destinations quickly, while others would leave during rush hour traffic and have a much longer drive. Still others would leave at different times with less extreme conditions. The average driving time gives you a rough idea of how long your drive will be, but without knowing what time you're leaving and what the conditions will be at that exact time, you could either arrive at the airport early or you could miss your flight entirely.

Figuring out how much money you need to be FI is similar. Stock markets are volatile. Interest rates change. The rate of inflation is variable. Just as there are times you can get to the airport faster than others, there are times when you can expect to spend more than 4 percent. Similarly, just as some people will sit in rush hour traffic, there will be times when you'll spend less than 4 percent.

If you are unlucky and retire at the wrong time and blindly withdraw from a portfolio when markets are down at the beginning of your retirement, there is a much greater chance that you'll run out of money in retirement. This is referred to as sequence of returns risk. We have to continue to learn, remain flexible, and adjust to conditions on the ground when we encounter them. ERN advises we use the "4 percent rule of thumb" to get started. Then we can reassess conditions as we get closer to the destination before making major financial decisions too early that could set us up for failure.

For me, the key to everything FI-related is flexibility and open-mindedness. This also holds true regarding my drawdown strategy once I'm past the point of FI where I'm no longer drawing income from my businesses.

*I don't want to be dogmatic about anything, which is why we call the so-called 4% Rule the "4 percent rule of thumb" here at **ChooseFI**. Sure, there's a high likelihood that the 4 percent drawdown strategy will succeed over thirty years or more, but I can't envision a scenario where I stick to it like clockwork regardless of real-life conditions.*

This is why I'm building in flexibility in two ways:

1. *I'm calculating my FI number at a more conservative 3.5 percent drawdown.*

2. *I'm building in a buffer when calculating my yearly expenses (the starting point of calculating your FI number) that would allow us to tighten the belt and cut out some fluff from our budget that wouldn't lessen our quality of life.*

While the 4% Rule is not perfect, using it as a guide provides a tangible target. The 4% Rule also has some other less obvious implications.

The 4% Rule is based on market returns over various periods. When you invest in index funds, you are accepting market returns rather than trying to beat the market. This is a wise decision. The majority of people who try to beat the market fail to do so. Therefore, if you are not an index fund investor, the assumptions of the 4% Rule research aren't valid.

The 4% Rule also has important implications related to investment fees. The average mutual fund charges annual fees of about 1 percent of assets each year. Investment advisory fees can also average 1 percent of assets per year. Investment fees are provided in percentages of assets rather than real dollars because they look so small. However, reframing investment expenses in the context of the 4% Rule means that someone paying "only" 2 percent of their portfolio in investment fees leaves only 2 percent left to support their lifestyle. Someone paying "only" 2 percent advisory fees who saves $1 million would only be able to spend $20,000 because the other $20,000 would go to pay investment fees. Someone in this scenario would actually need to save $2 million to provide a $40,000 income and pay $40,000 fees every year. Does that 1 to 2 percent still look like a little number?

When the 4% Rule and sequence of returns don't work in your favor, you may only want to take 3 percent from your portfolio. But paying fees of "only" 2 percent means two-thirds of your money goes to fees while being able to use only one third to support your lifestyle.

Index funds allow you to invest with minimal fees. A portfolio of index funds can be owned for 0.1 percent or less. On the same $1 million portfolio, a portfolio with 0.1 percent fees would cost only $1,000. Understanding the 4% Rule is a simple and powerful way to see the impact of seemingly small fees on your portfolio.

The 4% Rule not only emphasizes the importance of investing fees, it demonstrates the impact of your spending on achieving FI. Every $1,000 you spend annually requires you to accumulate $25,000 to support a 4 percent withdrawal rate. Taken a step further, every monthly expense requires you to save three hundred times that amount to support it *(25 x 12 = 300)*. Knowing this can be motivational when making spending decisions. Is it worth it to cut $100 from your monthly expenses by being more efficient with grocery shopping, dining out less, switching phone plans, or cutting cable? A hundred bucks doesn't sound like a lot, but reframe the question: Is it worth it to work long enough to save $30,000 more to go to a restaurant one night a month, have the most expensive phone plan, or keep cable TV? As a valuist, you have to answer that question. Understanding the impact of your spending on how quickly you can achieve FI may change that decision.

IS THE SIMPLE PATH FOR YOU?

This is not an investing book, and this chapter is meant to serve only as an introduction to investing in stocks and bonds using index funds. The point is that the technical aspects of investing that intimidate so many and prevent them from getting started are overblown. You can be a successful investor with just one index fund that you buy and hold forever. Many investors fail to get started or pay far too much for unnecessary financial advice and products.

Simultaneously, others fail as investors because they underestimate the emotional and behavioral aspects of investing. While investing is simple, it is not easy. You need to go in with eyes wide open before committing money so you'll avoid acting on the fear and greed that causes most investors' returns to be substantially less than their investments.

Many of the people you read about in this book, including me, got to FI by developing a high savings rate, then investing those savings in simple, passive, low-cost index funds. Many others fail because they don't understand the simple truths presented in this chapter.

ACTION STEPS

1. **Make a list of your recurring expenses.** (If you've started tracking or budgeting your spending as suggested in Chapter 4, this should be easy). Multiply your annual expenses by twenty-five or monthly expenses by three hundred to see the impact of your spending on the amount you need to accumulate to achieve FI. Does that spending add value to your life? Would your path to FI be shorter and easier if you didn't have to save the amount required to sustain that spending?

2. **Check your 401(k) and other investment accounts.** Calculate your investment fees including expense ratios. If you aren't sure how to do this, there are free online tools. Check the ChooseFI website for recommendations.

3. **Read a few books to get a deeper understanding of index investing.** For further reading on index investing start with JL Collins's *The Simple Path to Wealth* and John Bogle's *The Little Book of Common Sense Investing*. For further insight into index fund investing with more diverse asset allocation check out Rick Ferri's *All About Asset Allocation* and William Bernstein's *The Intelligent Asset Allocator*.

Entrepreneurs are the only people who will work 80 hours a week to avoid working 40 hours a week.

LORI GREINER

CHAPTER

13

BUILD A BUSINESS

When Brad and Jonathan interviewed Todd Tresidder of *Financial Mentor*, he emphasized the different investment paths available to those who *Choose FI*. He pointed out that starting a business is different from investing in paper assets or real estate. Investing in stocks, bonds, or real estate requires you to create or borrow capital to invest, but starting a business is different. Tresidder said, "In business, you're literally creating equity out of thin air."

At first glance, Tresidder's claim that you can create money out of thin air can seem too good to be true. But what does any successful business do? They add value that people are willing to pay for. It's not magic, voodoo, or a scam. The basic premise of the entire Make More section of this book is that an individual or business can create wealth by adding enough value that someone is willing to pay for the products or services you provide. A business can also serve as an investment that can further grow wealth that's been reinvested into the business.

Many people would love to start a business, but they think they need an innovative new idea, a lot of money, or a special talent, so they never get started. In reality, anyone can start a business. We all have interests, skills, and abilities in things other people can't or don't want to do.

You can literally start a business today. The only thing stopping you is you.

We don't have to look far for examples. Brad and Jonathan started the *ChooseFI* podcast with just a few hundred dollars and a lot of hard work. Within a year, the podcast was reaching tens of thousands of people every week and had enough momentum to give Jonathan the confidence to leave his six-figure salary as a pharmacist to pursue his dreams.

BUSINESS CHALLENGES

None of this is to say that the business path is easy. Each investment path that allows you to *Choose FI* has unique risks and challenges. The first challenge of investing in your own business, according to inventor, entrepreneur, and *Shark Tank* star Lori Greiner, is the willingness to work eighty hours for yourself to avoid working forty hours for "the man." Businesses can be a time suck if you don't manage your time well.

Robert Kiyosaki uses a unique framework to describe the ways we can make money in his book *Cashflow Quadrants*. He differentiates the self-employed (those who own a job) from business owners (those who own a system that works for them). When you create a business, it is hard work to get started. Kiyosaki's framework is helpful to avoid creating a situation of self-employment with the trappings of a job. These trappings include trading time for money on an ongoing basis and paying high income taxes while giving up the ability to leave work at work and receiving benefits like paid vacation and employer-subsidized health insurance. Kiyosaki's framework also emphasizes the importance of working on a business—developing systems that allow your business to make money without you—rather than working in the business, where the business stops earning when you stop working.

Another challenge of starting a business? There is no how-to manual. Alan Donegan, who coaches people to start businesses through the *PopUp Business School*, spoke about this with Brad and Jonathan. He said that you need to determine what to do each day and be motivated to do it. You also have to keep experimenting and innovating. Conditions will inevitably change, and you are responsible for figuring things out. In his experience, those motivated only by money don't last because they aren't willing to keep working through the challenges that will inevitably arise. Business owners who he's seen succeed are driven by a passion to use their businesses as vehicles to serve and help others. Brad's experience of failing repeatedly while chasing easy money but succeeding in his later businesses—where he focused on serving people in areas he had a genuine interest—is a perfect example of this.

There are several ways to use a business as an investment vehicle. One is to go all in on a business as your primary means of income and your primary investment vehicle. This can offer big rewards but comes with high risk.

Bobby Hoyt of *Millennial Money Man* discussed this path on the *ChooseFI* podcast. Hoyt tells the story of working hard to pay off student loan debt. He had planned to work another year to build a cash cushion before quitting his job as a school teacher and turning his website into his full-time gig. At the time, his site was not profitable. In fact, he'd made only a couple dollars and didn't have a plan to monetize it. He discussed his idea with an entrepreneurial family friend who advised him that if he was serious, he needed to do it immediately.

Hoyt discussed the idea with his wife that night, and then promptly walked into his boss's office the next day and quit his secure teaching job to become an entrepreneur. He noted that while it sounds like a cool and "ballsy" story, he awoke in the middle of the night feeling like his heart was going to explode out of his chest. He ran into the bathroom, looked in the mirror, and thought he was going to die from a panic attack that continued for about a half hour before he was able to calm down. Revealing that he put all his eggs in one basket and quit his job without a solid plan, he warns, "I never recommend that other people do that."

Rowing to shore, then burning the boats is the way many view entrepreneurship. It makes "success" more likely because failure is not an option. Because there is no fallback option, "success" can be the result of eighteen-hour work days, working months or even years without a day off, or going into debt to keep things afloat.

We see variations of this storyline where we glorify the entrepreneur who risked everything, lived on a couch in the office, and almost gave up before finally making it big and creating a billion-dollar company.

This storyline overlooks two key points.

You don't have to create a billion-dollar company, or even a million-dollar company to have a successful business and reach FI.

It also contains a massive selection bias, focusing on the "unicorn" who made it while ignoring the many others who, despite taking risks, fail anyway.

Hoyt was a success story. He now has months when his website makes several times more than he made in a year as a school teacher. But things could have gone the other way. Investing in your own business can have this type of variability, causing many to shy away. But is the risk of failing reason enough not to try?

Jonathan went all in on the business path, quitting his professional job to focus on *ChooseFI* full-time. Even his partner Brad said he was a bit taken aback when Jonathan informed him of this decision. At the time, their combined business income was not as much as Jonathan was making as a pharmacist.

Jonathan's efficiency with spending enabled him to pay off $168,000 of student loan debt in four years, and that translated to risk reduction when he started his business. If he still had student loan payments, car payments, and credit card payments due each month, as is common for many taking the standard path through life, his decision would have been much riskier. Throw a small business loan on top of that, and it's easy to see why so many find starting a business intimidating.

Brad and Jonathan applied lean start-up principles to *ChooseFI*. They spent a few dollars for a web domain and bought a couple of microphones. Then they used their laptops and sweat equity to get their business off the ground. When you take this approach to business and life, you have tremendous freedom to try new things without taking a financial risk, even if you are still early on the road to FI. If *ChooseFI* had crashed and burned, Jonathan would have been all right. Nobody wants to fail, and it wouldn't have been fun, but no one would have been knocking on his door to repossess his car or collect other debts. He would have probably just been heading back to a pharmacy job, and he'd have had the satisfaction of knowing he tried. If you try and it doesn't work out, you haven't failed, you've just gained a learning experience. Framed that way, his decision wasn't very risky at all.

You realize the benefits of FI long before you reach FI. We call this a fully funded lifestyle change (FFLC), and this is really my story. I got my expenses down to the bone and paid off all my debt. So when we started this podcast on the side, there was zero risk.

*There came a time when I had to choose between the podcast and keeping my pharmacy job. The podcast had started to produce enough income to pay my bills, which were low because of my prior choices and actions. I also had several years of expenses saved up. These circumstances enabled me to go all in on **ChooseFI**. I got to design my future long before I actually reached FI.*

JONATHAN

*At first, when Jonathan told me he was going to quit his safe, six-figure job as a pharmacist to pursue **ChooseFI** full-time, I was really surprised and a little worried. But I quickly realized this was **exactly** what we were describing on our podcast: control your expenses so your life just structurally doesn't cost that much, find a passion project that you want to pour your heart and soul into, limit the downside by always having options (he planned to keep his pharmacy certifications), and most of all, take action to make your life better and more fulfilling. Jonathan did all those things, and the success of **ChooseFI** since then is directly tied to the time, effort, and love he has put into growing this movement.*

Tresidder considers the business path to be the least risky way to achieve FI. He said, "You can manage risk so tightly in business, even when I fail, I usually profit." He explained that by controlling risk so tightly, "you can fail ninety-nine times and on the one-hundredth try, be financially independent. Or you can get it right the first time. There's no compound wealth equation involved." He added that it's not rare to become financially independent quickly by building a business. "It happens all the time."

Alan Donegan echoes these points. He often sees the misconception that starting a business has to be risky when teaching aspiring entrepreneurs in the *PopUp Business School*. He sees two things that stop people from starting a business. First, they don't have the money to do it. Second, they don't have the confidence to try.

There's a common belief that it takes money to make money. Donegan observes this is taught in business schools and is reinforced by popular TV shows like *The Apprentice, Shark Tank,* and *Dragon's Den*. He said the traditional model is you write a business plan, borrow money, and spend the money to get the business going. Then you go out and try to sell your ideas, services, or products. Of course, this scares people and sounds risky. That's why he teaches people to do the exact opposite: flip the traditional business model on its head just like we do with conventional personal finance wisdom when we *Choose FI*.

The traditional business model ends with the sale. To do the opposite, we start with sales. Donegan stresses that to get an honest opinion, you need to ask people to buy something. Up until that point they will be nice to you. He said, "If you ask for the sale, you'll get the real response. And if you get the sale before you go into debt, you can start your business without risk, because if they say yes, you're going. You've got an order. Your business is running. If they say no, you've lost nothing."

There's a common misconception that if you build it, they will come. Donegan emphasizes that if you build it, no one will come until you market it and sell it. Even then, they may not buy. This is why he starts with sales to limit downside risk.

This theme was emphasized by other guests on the *ChooseFI* podcast who took the entrepreneurial path. Dominick Quartuccio, the life coach and author of the book *Design Your Future*, shared his approach with Brad and Jonathan: "When I have a new concept, I bring it out, and I start to sell it, and I find out how much people are willing to pay for it, and if it's even a concept that's worth pursuing."

Brandon Pearce, the location-independent entrepreneur, developed online software that solved his problems of scheduling music lessons and collecting payments from students. When he told other music teachers about it, he got positive feedback. Here's how he described the start of his business to Brad and Jonathan: "It took me a few weeks to put a payment page up, but that's really all it took for me to start seeing if other teachers were really interested in this. And sales started coming in, and I realized that I was onto something. I think after the first sale, I mean I knew right away as soon as someone is willing to pay for it, well certainly there are other people who are willing to pay for it. And that's all it took." Over several years, Pearce built this software into a location-independent business to serve the needs of music teachers. His business allowed him to travel the world with his family. He shared on the podcast, "we've been traveling the world now for eight years, been to thirty-six countries as a family, and are just trying to live life now."

The next thing Donegan stresses to decrease risk when starting a business is focusing on starting it for as little money as possible. His reasoning is simple: If you don't borrow or spend a lot of your own money, there is less reason to be scared. Remember the two things that stop most people from starting a business—the belief that it takes a lot of money and a lack of confidence. If you can start a business for little or no money, you've killed both birds with one stone.

Donegan stresses doing whatever you can to start your business with no start-up costs. He noted multiple ways to do this, including finding ways to get as much as possible for free through available resources, borrowing things for little or no cost, and bartering instead of spending money. He also advises selling your value before you create it, noting that if you can build trust, you can ask for payment before creating and delivering your product or service. He said it's possible to build any type of business while starting with nothing. "I've seen restaurants built for free. I've seen physical businesses built with bricks and mortar built for free. I've seen websites and online businesses built for free. In fact, I haven't found a single business yet that you can't start for free."

SIDE HUSTLES AND ENCORE CAREERS

For some, going all in on a business still feels risky. This is where many in the FI community incorporate a side hustle. A side hustle is an additional income stream you can pursue without giving up your nine-to-five job. This adds another element of safety because even if the side hustle goes completely sideways, you still have your day job. Side hustles allow you to pursue your passions even if there isn't an obvious or immediate way to make them financially lucrative. A side hustle can simply be a part-time job, whether self-employed or employed by someone else. Either can be a good way to shorten your path to FI, but a job requires continued work to have continued income. Developing your side hustle into a business allows you to utilize systems that create cash flow that doesn't require you to trade time for money directly. A side hustle can start simply and grow into a business as you grow, learn, and figure out how to scale.

There are several applications of the side hustle for those who *Choose FI*. The first is for those with a low income or who are working themselves out of debt and having difficulty creating margin in their lives with their normal income. A side hustle can provide that margin and break the cycle of the paycheck-to-paycheck struggle. The second application is for those already on the path to FI. A side hustle can make an already high savings rate even higher, shortening the path to FI. For those who are close to FI, the income from a side hustle can also provide the courage to take the leap from the security of a job with a steady income and a high savings rate into the unknown of retirement.

Brad is an example of someone already on the path to FI who accelerated that journey with side hustles. He developed skills experimenting with online businesses, taking small risks while learning. He began to have modest financial success with his blog *Richmond Savers*, and then more success with his web-based business *Travel Miles 101*. The additional security of his side hustle income gave him the freedom he wouldn't have otherwise felt to take the leap and leave his career as an accountant at thirty-five years old.

Another option is to start a business after achieving FI and leaving your career. This is the path I have taken. I saw the potential benefits of starting a side hustle business while working, but I was already saving around 60 percent of my income and was well on the path to FI when I started to consider this option. At that point, it made more sense for me to continue focusing on my career while spending my free time with my wife and young child rather than working more to try to make additional income.

Now that I'm no longer working in my original career, I can devote all my energy to pursuing a business. This has several benefits. The first is an increased feeling of financial security. It's one thing to understand the 4% Rule and the mathematical chance you won't run out of money while taking withdrawals from your portfolio in retirement. It's something totally different to actually experience the psychological shift of going from someone saving a high percentage of their income to someone suddenly depleting assets. This often traps many people in the "one more year" syndrome because they're never quite sure they have enough money saved up, so they keep going to a job to build a bigger cushion—just for one more year. Then another. And another. Just in case.

Once people leave the workforce, they can go from a feeling of living with abundance due to their high savings rate to living with a scarcity mindset. Earning some income after achieving FI eliminates a lot of these fears and insecurities and allows you to continue living with an abundance mindset.

There are benefits beyond money for those who start a business after achieving FI. Many people start down the path to FI focused on retirement because they want freedom from a job they dislike. Once they get there, some find retirement isn't all it's cracked up to be. Retirees often feel a societal disconnect, which can contribute to depression and a variety of other physical and mental health issues. An "encore career" as an entrepreneur can provide motivation and purpose for your life while allowing you to work on things you're passionate about and enjoy. This provides a great way to gain the benefit of owning a business without the risk typically associated with entrepreneurship.

DESIGN YOUR LIFESTYLE

Brad and Jonathan had an interesting exchange when they talked to both Barney of *The Escape Artist* and Alan Donegan from *PopUp Business School* on Episode 49 of the *ChooseFI* podcast. Barney and Alan were on the podcast together to discuss the British perspective on FI. Each had different career paths that contributed to their unique perspectives. Barney opined, "You can essentially go one of two ways. You can either choose a job that you love, or you can choose a job that pays really, really well. Either of those, to my mind, are rational choices. With the former, you in some ways don't need to get to financial independence. If you genuinely have a job that you love and you'd kind of almost do it unpaid, but you get paid for it, that's great. You've solved the puzzle . . . The alternative is to do what I did, which is to choose a well-paid job."

Donegan disagreed. "I don't think it's always mutually exclusive. I do think you can find work that you love that does pay. There are people who do it. It's just not the norm. I do think a lot of people just settle. They settle for these jobs that are around me." He added, "There's always other options, such as creating your own work."

Tim Ferriss popularized the idea of lifestyle design in his book *The 4-Hour Work Week*. The ideas in his book can seem a bit far-fetched when viewed from the standard path. But as you step back and view entrepreneurship through the eyes of someone pursuing FI, combining business strategies discussed in this chapter with the lifestyle choices discussed in earlier sections, it becomes apparent that the lifestyle you desire is possible for most of us, if not all of us. It's also less risky than most assume. Investing in your own business at any stage of the process is a powerful tool that can help make the life of your dreams a reality.

ACTION STEPS

1. **Identify where you are on the path to FI.** Consider ways you could utilize a business to accelerate your path to FI, improve your lifestyle, or do both simultaneously.

2. **As you consider business ideas, think about what you would need to get that business started.** Brainstorm ways to obtain everything you would need for free.

3. **Analyze your business or the one you are considering.** Is it really a business/investment or are you creating a job? Start developing systems so the business is not dependent on your presence to operate.

There have been few things in my life which have had a more genial effect on my mind than the possession of a piece of land.

HARRIET MARTINEAU

CHAPTER

14

INVEST IN REAL ESTATE

Investors commonly compare investing in paper assets (i.e., stocks and bonds) with real estate to convince others that one path is better than the other. It's like debating whether apples are better than oranges. It's an impossible argument. They're just different. Real estate provides a hybrid investment path combining the characteristics of passive investments with the characteristics of a business or a job.

Your efforts can add value just as with any other business investment. Let's start by looking at two elements of real estate investing that can enable you to get higher returns than might be expected with passive investments: sweat equity and leverage.

SWEAT EQUITY

A key feature of using real estate as an investment vehicle is increased control over your outcomes. Chad "Coach" Carson went all in on real estate, using it both to make a living and as his primary investment vehicle to build wealth. His success enabled him to reach FI in his mid-thirties. He sees this increased control over your outcomes as a double-edged sword. The benefit of having more control is that you can reach FI sooner. You just have to work harder, learn faster, and keep hustling. The flip side is that everything goes through you. You have to be willing to put in the work. You have to add value to each deal. This can be intimidating to a new real estate investor, unsure where to get started.

Carson noted that real estate investing doesn't have to be an all-or-nothing path. Many people can benefit from owning just one or two investment properties. Once owned free and clear, they can produce several thousand dollars per month. Combined with a low-cost lifestyle, this could be enough to allow someone to be FI or at least reduce the burden on their passive investment accounts by producing steady monthly income. Combining real estate investing with the FI mindset differentiates this path of investing from what many real estate investors do. Many are constantly looking for the next deal, taking on tremendous amounts of risky debt in the process with no endgame in sight. They build large portfolios but remain trapped on the standard path.

Carson feels fortunate to have learned this valuable lesson early as a real estate investor. He said,

"Some of the best mentors I've had in real estate said just keep it simple.

Buy a house a year for five years and make each deal better than the last one. Don't try to be fancy. Don't try to be crazy. Just try to do the fundamentals really, really well." This idea of aggregating marginal gains is certainly not foreign to those who *Choose FI*. This mindset has allowed Carson to consistently make better deals, focusing on strategies he's most comfortable with and has found to be successful.

The simple strategy of gradually accumulating properties has been effective for others in the FI community. One example is Scott Trench, author of *Set for Life* and co-host of the podcast *BiggerPockets Money*. On the *ChooseFI* podcast, he told Brad and Jonathan that he bought his first investment property, a duplex, as a "house hack" in fall 2014. He repeated the process, moving into a second duplex. He then purchased a quadplex the next time. Throughout the process, he was able to get favorable owner-occupied financing and a cheap or free place to live. These purchases gave him seven rental units plus a place to live at the end of the four years. This simple approach to real estate investing helped propel him toward financial independence by the time he was in his late twenties.

Carson explained that there are two parts to finding good deals. He said most of us are good at the first one without needing much experience. It is qualitatively finding a good home in a good neighborhood. His rule of thumb is to find a house in a neighborhood where he would want to live. He said, "Buying or renting a home to live in is an emotional decision, so you make money in real estate by delivering a product that has emotional appeal because living in a home is emotional." The other half of the equation is quantitative. You have to do your homework to learn the market where you want to invest, understand financing, then put it all together to know if a deal will be profitable while delivering value to others. Carson said being a successful real estate investor means you have to be a "walking dichotomy"—balancing emotions and math all the time.

LEVERAGE

Real estate allows you to leverage your specific skills, interests, and talents, adding value to deals to increase returns. This can be done in several ways. You can focus on a particular neighborhood, or even a particular street and become an expert in a tiny market. This can enable you to spot a deal quickly. You could become a real estate agent to give yourself more access to deals, also allowing you to decrease or eliminate commissions on transactions. If you're handy, you can buy a run-down property and bring it up to standard for the neighborhood. You can add value by adding a bedroom or bathroom to make a property even more appealing to a renter or buyer. You could combine these strategies. Adding value through sweat equity has endless possibilities, allowing greater returns than are possible with passive investments without having to take on more financial risk.

Sweat equity allows you to leverage increased investment returns by applying more effort. Leveraging debt to buy properties also enables you to increase investment returns. But debt isn't a free lunch, either. It can add an element of risk to your investments.

Why would you want to take the risk of using financial leverage? The first reason to use debt is that it may allow you to enter the game. You can buy index mutual funds or ETFs for $100 or less. You can start many businesses for free. Real estate is different. Even a "cheap" property can cost tens of thousands of dollars, and in many areas starter homes cost well over $100,000. The cost of entry can be a high barrier to get over for many people. Using debt allows you to commit a small amount of your own money to control an asset worth much more.

Even if you can buy real estate with cash, using debt can make it far more profitable. Assume you could purchase a house for $100,000 and make a $5,000 profit over one year, this would be a 5 percent return on investment (ROI). But what if you use leverage? If you could put down only 20 percent, or $20,000, and still make $5,000, you've made a 25 percent ROI on the same deal. Instead of tying up your own money to purchase the asset, you can use your tenant's rent money to pay down your mortgage.

Buying leveraged real estate is a tax-efficient way to build wealth. If you don't use leverage, you need to save after-tax dollars to purchase a property. The rent you collect on these paid-off homes would then be mostly profit, which is also taxable income. Using financial leverage allows you to invest less of your own after-tax dollars. You then apply a portion of the rental income to the business expense of paying interest on this debt, which is not taxable. This allows you to accumulate wealth while limiting your tax burden. *(Note: These tax benefits are specific to the US tax code. Laws in other countries may vary.)*

This is just the beginning of what leverage can give you when building wealth. If you could buy five leveraged deals identical to the first, your $100,000 could give you control of $500,000 worth of real estate. Instead of making one deal with a 5 percent return, leverage gives you the opportunity to make five deals. Instead of using $100,000 to make $5,000 in a year without leverage, you've used the same $100,000 to make $25,000! Alternatively, you could buy just one leveraged deal and leave the remaining money to support your lifestyle, invest passively in index funds, or pursue other more profitable business options.

It's easy to see why leverage can be addictive and how many people get themselves in trouble with debt. Todd Tresidder of *Financial Mentor* discussed this risk with Brad and Jonathan on the *ChooseFI* podcast. He pointed out, "Financial leverage is the only type of leverage that cuts both ways. It can kill you if you get it wrong, and it can make you very wealthy when you get it right."

One upside of owning real estate is that housing prices and rents tend to match or outpace the rate of inflation (i.e., an ongoing increase in prices). This means the same amount of money in the future will have less buying power than it does today. Leveraged real estate is a bet on continued inflation. Leverage makes sense when the underlying asset continues to go up in value.

You may also experience deflation, where people have less incentive to buy today because a property is likely to be cheaper tomorrow. Leverage combined with deflation can be devastating. This happened in the financial crisis of 2008 and 2009. There was a panic, banks stopped lending money, and deflation destroyed real estate prices. This left many people, both real estate investors and homeowners alike, underwater on their mortgages. They owed more money on their properties than the properties were worth, making it difficult to sell the properties and pay off the debt. When you're underwater on a property, you have to pay the difference between the amount you owe and the current value of the house just to have someone take it off your hands.

While many people allow the risk of leveraging debt to scare them out of investing in real estate, most are comfortable using debt to purchase residential real estate. Maybe that's because they don't understand the risk involved.

USING FI PRINCIPLES TO MANAGE DEBT

While leveraging debt adds risk to your finances, you can minimize that risk by having the mindset of someone on the path to FI. Scott Trench illustrated this to Brad and Jonathan through his example of buying his first "house hack" and contrasting it with a "normal" home purchase by someone on the standard path.

Trench bought his first duplex in the Denver area for $240,000 with only 5 percent down ($12,000). Tenants on one side paid $1,150 per month in rent, and he had a roommate living with him and paying him rent. These rents covered his mortgage payment every month. Eliminating his own housing expense allowed him to develop a high savings rate quickly. According to Trench, housing costs represent about 35 percent of spending for the average American household.

Trench contrasted this against a hypothetical purchase of a similar $240,000 single-family residence with the same 5 percent down payment made by someone taking the standard path through life. They would have a monthly mortgage payment of about $1,550 each month.

He then gave the example of a real estate crisis where housing prices and rents drop by 30 percent overnight. Even in this worst-case scenario, Trench could still use his reduced rents to cover most of his mortgage while paying only a couple hundred dollars a month to continue living in this property. He could ride out a down cycle with little difficulty.

The person on the standard path would have to continue paying $1,550 each month, even if they lost their job and couldn't afford that payment. They would have a difficult time selling the house if needed because they would be under water. We saw this time and again in the financial crisis of 2008 and 2009. Yet people continue to take the standard path through life and take this risk every day.

If I could go back and change a single financial choice that I made in the past, it would be with regards to real estate. In particular, I wish I'd pursued house hacking.

College, or your early twenties, seems like the perfect opportunity to deploy this technique. You are used to sharing space anyways. Why not use it as an opportunity to accelerate your path to FI and get some landlord experience in the process. Both Scott Trench and Chad Carson benefited from this strategy. It's pretty evident that individuals who figure this out and execute it well set themselves up to be years ahead on their path to FI.

This single decision can create the margin of a 50 percent savings rate on nearly any income. While this lever isn't limited to college-age kids, it seems like a near-perfect situation and will likely be a rite of passage for my kids, one I'm excited to help them navigate.

JONATHAN

Anyone can become a real estate investor while controlling risk. Leveraged investment debt can actually be less risky than what people on the standard path take with a standard home purchase. And those on the standard path take this risk without the upside real estate investors have.

In his experience working for BiggerPockets, a real estate investing educational company, Trench reports being frustrated seeing people who have no income, no assets, and years of bad personal financial behavior turn to real estate investing thinking it will be their cure-all. He suggests they forget this approach and take a completely different view of real estate investing. He told Brad and Jonathan, "You have to get your financial house in order first, and then invest from a position of financial strength in order to accelerate your position."

In my mid-twenties I was burned badly on some real estate "investments" that, with the benefit of hindsight, were not investments at all but just speculative gambling. This soured me for a long time on real estate investing. But people like Scott Trench, Chad Carson, and Paula Pant, who writes the blog and hosts the podcast Afford Anything, have opened my eyes to approaching real estate investing as a true business where you aren't looking for appreciation of your home price (speculation you can't control), but a true business entity that runs off sound financial practices.

This simple mindset shift has given me the nerve to start investing in real estate again, and I'm excited about the possibilities!

TAX ADVANTAGES

Another advantage of investing in real estate is that it allows you to build wealth in a tax-efficient way. Leveraged real estate allows you to use other people's money to buy properties rather than having to save your after-tax income to build wealth.

The major tax advantage of investing in real estate rental properties is depreciation, a "paper expense" that is allowed by the IRS for accounting purposes. US tax law requires residential rental real estate to be depreciated over twenty-seven and a half years. This gives you an annual deduction on your tax form that offsets some taxable income that year, decreasing your tax bill. The additional tax benefit of real estate investments provides another way to spend less on taxes, allowing you to save more and accelerate the path to FI.

THE SIMPLE MATH OF REAL ESTATE

We refer to using index fund investing as the simple path to investing because it is passive and requires minimal effort. This implies that starting a business and investing in real estate are complex ventures. In some ways, this is true. During the accumulation phase, business and real estate paths require more thought and effort than passive index fund investing.

As we approach FI, the simple path becomes more complex. We use the 4% Rule to determine how much you need to be FI when taking the simple path with your investments. The 4% Rule relies on making assumptions about investment returns, interest rates, and inflation. These factors are unpredictable and out of your control. This makes the simple path complex and can be scary for those preparing to take the leap from a regular income to living off investments.

In contrast, real estate math becomes much simpler as you approach FI. Here is Carson's method for planning the transition from living off earned income to living off income produced by a real estate portfolio:

- Start with your number. What kind of budget would it take to be financially independent? How much income would it take to cover your family's expenses and provide the lifestyle you desire without needing to earn an income any longer?

- Once you have that number, the goal is to acquire enough real estate to produce this amount in a low risk, passive way. Carson favors having free and clear rental properties to provide this income with minimal risk, effort, and hassle. From there you simply develop a plan to achieve the minimal number of properties it takes to produce the income you need.

Of course, Carson is a real estate guy who makes a living investing in real estate and teaching others to follow him down this path. It's natural to be skeptical when he makes things sound so simple. Listen to what Karsten "Big ERN" Jeske of *Early Retirement Now* had to say about real estate in Episode 52R. Big ERN has a Ph.D. in finance and is bullish on stocks. He said, "Real estate is a very attractive asset class in retirement because you generate inflation-protected cash flow, and if your portfolio is diversified enough it's a reliable and predictable income stream. So if someone has a real estate portfolio and it generates, say 5 percent net rental income after subtracting costs for maintenance, repairs, property management, vacancies, and so on, and that cash flow pays for retirement expenses, then you can retire with what is effectively a 5 percent withdrawal rate. Most importantly, you never touch your principal. So that solves the problem of sequence of returns risk. So having some of our assets in real estate should be a wise move in retirement."

Once you've decided to invest in real estate, you'll need to develop a strategy for your investments. We've focused a lot on house hacking in this book because it ties in with other aspects of *Choosing FI*. It is also a low-risk, beginner-friendly way to dip your toes into real estate investing. This is not to imply that you have to house hack or that this is the only path to real estate investing.

Real estate investment options include single-family homes, duplexes, triplexes, quads, larger apartment buildings, commercial real estate, land, and vacation rentals, among others. You could buy properties with the intention of holding them forever, do quick flips, or any number of intermediate strategies. You may decide to be a lender to other real estate investors. There are many options for real estate investing, but exploring them in detail is beyond the scope of this chapter.

If you are looking to take a deeper dive into this topic, the two people featured in this chapter offer great resources to marry the concepts of real estate investing and FI. I recommend picking up Chad Carson's *Retire Early with Real Estate* and Scott Trench's *Set for Life* to learn more about ideas introduced in this chapter.

ACTION STEPS

1. **Look at your living expenses.** How much income do you need to support your lifestyle? Determine how many free-and-clear rental properties you would need to produce that amount of income.

2. **Analyze your rent or housing payment.** Determine how long you could maintain it if you lost your current income. Is your current housing situation putting you at financial risk? Could you use your housing as an investment to help build wealth and simultaneously decrease financial risk?

3. **Start taking a thirty- to sixty-minute daily walk around where you live and/or work.** While getting exercise, note how many properties are currently for sale or rent. Start getting a sense of your local market. What do properties cost? What do they rent for? How long do they take to sell? Pay attention to what makes some properties more attractive than others. As you do this, start to think about ways you could add value to real estate deals. Are you handy? Do you have cash that could enable you to buy properties quickly at discounts? Do you have access to favorable financing? Could you find good deals for other investors for a small profit?

PART 5

WHAT'S NEXT

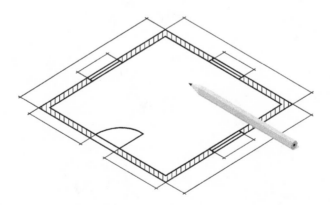

You are the sum total of everything you've ever seen, heard, eaten, smelled, been told, forgot—it's all there. Everything influences each of us, and because of that I try to make sure that my experiences are positive.

MAYA ANGELOU

CHAPTER

15

ENJOY THE JOURNEY

The conventional wisdom is that we need to work our entire adult lives so we can retire in our sixties or seventies. We're told it's difficult to obtain FI. Many people never do.

The FI community flips conventional wisdom on its head. It's not uncommon for those in the FI community to achieve FI in only ten to fifteen years. Some do it in less than a decade. While this can be inspirational, it can also give the false impression that the path to FI is easy. It's not.

Many on the path to FI, or those who have already achieved it, demonstrate a common pattern. We start off frustrated with the standard path through life, so we get excited about the idea of FIRE. We see a lack of money keeping us bound to jobs, which prevent us from living the lifestyles we desire. We become certain we'll be happy once we have enough money to become FI and retire. All we need to do is put our heads down and get through that decade or two of work to reach the promised land. In the process, we fail to enjoy the journey.

Fortunately, enough people have shared their own version of this story that you can learn without repeating our mistakes.

You should enjoy the progressive freedom and power you gain on the path to FI.

But this is often easier said than done. Let's look at why people struggle, then explore ideas from the FI community that enable you to enjoy the journey to FI.

In Chapter 2 we briefly introduced Jeff, *The Happy Philosopher*, a physician who was burning out only a few years into his career. Discovering FI was an awakening for him. He was initially under the impression that he needed over ten million dollars to retire. He quickly realized that his personal FI number was a small fraction of this, and with his high salary he could hit his target in about five years. Solving the financial portion of FI was relatively easy for him. But this did not solve his primary problem. He described feeling burned out and dissatisfied with his work and life, and he still had what he described as a "five-year prison sentence" until he could get out. He realized he had to learn to be happy now.

It's easy to get caught up thinking we would be happy if we just had a little more fame, knowledge, power, prestige, or stuff. Some in the FI community think more money is all we need. Jeff discovered happiness for him can be having less and learning to say no.

Jeff used the analogy of kittens and alligators to describe his approach to decluttering his life in the quest for happiness. Kittens are cute, cuddly, playful creatures that bring happiness while alligators are ugly, menacing, and nasty. If we had a room filled with kittens and alligators and wanted to make it a more peaceful and happy place, we couldn't just add more kittens—they would only provide more food for the gators. It would make for an ugly scene. The obvious place to start would be removing the alligators. However, we rarely recognize this in our daily lives.

Jeff focused on eliminating the things that were detracting from his life rather than trying to add more of the things that we often think will make us happy. He eliminated unnecessary obligations that slipped onto the calendar. He quit watching cable news, which caused anxiety and stress. He resolved to reduce his workload, cutting down to half time, even though it meant taking a financial hit that slowed his time to FI.

Jeff's transition from full-time to part-time work took three years to complete. He said going part-time was his worst financial decision because a physician's ability to generate income is their greatest asset. Still, he said it was a really great personal decision. He also noted that because of other changes he made during the transition to part-time work, he became much happier even while still working full-time.

Brandon, who writes *The Mad Fientist* blog, shared a similar story of unhappiness on his path to FI. I related to his story on an intensely personal level. *The Mad Fientist* was one of the first blogs I ever read, and I still read every word Brandon writes. I credit his blog with simplifying the US tax code for me and making it interesting, things I previously thought were impossible. His writing helped me optimize my path to FI, giving me years of additional financial freedom by making simple planning changes.

Brandon's writing changed my life for the better, but reading his blog was also the biggest reason for my unhappiness on the path to FI. He frequently wrote about optimizing the path to FI with the underlying assumptions that once you achieve FI and retire, your life will dramatically improve. The sooner you get there, the better. Comparing my investing and tax planning mistakes against his "optimized" path left me with a lot of regrets. Focusing on how great FIRE would be made it difficult for me to enjoy the amazing life I already had.

Brandon discussed his own struggles with Brad and Jonathan on the *ChooseFI* podcast. Listening to Brandon describe his own journey and feelings of unhappiness on his path to FI was very powerful. He said, "I was so hyper-focused on reaching financial independence, nothing else mattered." He couldn't have fun. He analyzed every dollar he spent and thought about how much money he could be saving and how it could allow him to retire sooner. In the process, he isolated himself for about two years.

Brandon's mindset affected his wife as well. She moved to the United States from her native country of Scotland to be with him. He said, "Here she is in a foreign country and . . . all her husband wants to do is read tax documents." Brandon didn't see how bad things became until she told him she thought he was depressed and pointed out that neither of them was happy. He quickly decided to make changes. He couldn't put off happiness until he was FI. The things most important to him could be lost by then if he didn't change. They decided to move to Scotland to be closer to her family and started doing things with their friends and family again.

Brandon eventually hit his FI number. Although he was still working, he'd already become a happier person. Achieving FI didn't change anything. He said, "I've been planning for this and putting off happiness until I hit this goal and now I hit it, and it's like . . . nothing is different." Looking back, it was obvious. Having an extra dollar in your bank account doesn't magically change things. It's a powerful lesson to heed as we go about building happier lives on the journey to FI.

EMBRACE YOUR MISTAKES

A lot of my unhappiness on the path to FI came as a result of comparing myself to others in the FI community. While the stories in this book can be inspirational, they can also lead you to play "what if?" while dwelling on past mistakes. In my case, I did most of the things others on more optimal paths were doing, often as well or better than they did. At the same time, my wife and I made massive investing and tax-planning mistakes. We blindly trusted an advisor who put his interests ahead of our own, causing us to pay unnecessary fees and taxes that lengthened the journey to FI by years. I was bitter and regretful that I hadn't taken the time to educate myself sooner.

J.D. Roth was one of the first successful personal finance bloggers. He's now part of the FI community, but he didn't start there. Roth's popularity as a blogger is most attributable to his willingness to share his personal journey getting out of debt and his past full of financial mistakes, which many people can relate to. When he talked with Brad and Jonathan on the podcast, he shared the following insights: "You have to recognize that not everyone starts at the same place, and you're going to have bad things happen to you. But when the bad things happen, you have to have the resilience to say, OK, yeah this happened. It sucks, but I'm going to move forward and here's how I'm going to solve it."

Much of my solution to becoming happier and enjoying my homestretch to FI was the decision to use my investing and tax planning mistakes as inspiration to start writing about my own journey. I became a consumer advocate focused on helping others avoid repeating my experience, turning the negative into a positive expression of my passion for helping others.

Jonathan shared a similar theme when discussing his journey to overcome his six-figure student loan debt on the path to FI.

Though he spent years working on getting out from under that debt, he said, "I don't regret my past decisions for a minute." Those experiences have become his story and a driving force behind creating and growing *ChooseFI* as a platform to expose others to a better way of life.

> *Many of us start our journeys to FI fed up by stress, busyness, and general discontent with a life that revolves around going to a job to make money. So without much thought, we desire the opposite—retirement.*

When Fritz Gilbert of The *Retirement Manifesto* spoke with Brad and Jonathan on the podcast, he asked, "How much more interesting would your job be if you're just doing it because you want to do it?" Work provides a lot of the things that make us happy, from income to personal development to providing an outlet to serve others, giving meaning and purpose to our lives. Fritz said that as you contemplate this, you realize, "The work that you thought sucked so much doesn't suck so much anymore."

Many in the FI community have come to the same conclusion. We continue to do meaningful and paid work in "retirement" even though we don't really need the money. Some criticize people who write about FIRE, saying we're "not really retired." *Mr. Money Mustache* labels these people the "Internet Retirement Police." They find it offensive that we don't meet their definition of retirement (i.e., stopping paid work entirely). They imply that people who talk about FIRE are frauds. They say it doesn't make sense to do what it takes to *Choose FI*. Why bother saving if you're going to keep working anyway?

Early retirement is very different from traditional retirement. It's not about what you are running from, but what you are running to. It's not about never working again but claiming autonomy, mastery, and purpose for your life. You get to pick and choose the activities that light you up and design a future you can get excited about without the risk or fear of how you'll keep the lights on or feed your family. Imagine not being motivated by profits or scared of failure. Maybe you join or create a start-up. Maybe you purchase a farm with your family or travel overseas and write about your adventure. Create a movie script or a children's book. Learn to paint . . . or set up a ministry in a developing country.

What do you want to do?

REDEFINE RETIREMENT

It's odd that people have strong attachments to the idea of what retirement should be. Retirement just became common in the past century, made possible by a combination of increased life expectancy and increased productivity. Before that, workers didn't retire. People worked until they died or until they were physically unable to work, at which point they were supported by their families.

When retirement was introduced, workers didn't choose to retire. Employers made the choice for them in order to make room for more productive workers. It's analogous to the way I retire a pair of old socks with a hole because they're no longer useful. Retirement was dreaded. It meant you were reaching the end of your useful life.

The finance industry seized on the opportunity to define retirement as a time of leisure. They could help you save and plan for this new phase of life. It's difficult to find a retirement planning commercial or brochure without a couple walking on a beach or a group playing golf. But is that what retirement has to be?

We need to redefine what retirement means and should be. Or maybe scrap the idea of retirement completely and focus on building lives we don't want to retire from. This is why we focus so much on the idea of FI, while not spending much time on the idea of retirement. For me, FI is all about having the freedom to spend my time and energy on the things I want to do; my financial concerns are secondary. FI is about being able to incorporate meaningful work into my life rather than trying to squeeze in life around my job.

Jonathan described FI as having the freedom to fail. He said FI is defined by "the fact that you no longer have to work for money. In many cases, you find that you have the option to make more money because you're able to take risks that you wouldn't have considered in a more conservative nine-to-five, addicted to W-2 income era of your life." He added, "Work doesn't have to be related to earning. Freedom to fail allows you to pursue something that you love." This circles back to the entrepreneurial spirit that leads many to invest in their own business at different stages on their path to FI, without the risk and associated fears that trap many on the standard path.

Brad thinks FI is about even more than the freedom to fail: FI gives you the freedom to explore. Once you have the financial part down, you can take a step back and look at your life holistically. This is where life gets interesting because you can start asking bigger questions. What do I get value out of? What do I enjoy? What would make me happier? How can I progress to bring me value in the future?

The word retirement is so loaded with negative connotations of either sitting around watching TV or sipping umbrella drinks and watching the world go by that I choose not to focus so much on the early retirement aspect of the FIRE acronym and instead focus mainly on FI.

What FI means to me is an entire world of possibilities and the ability to spend my most precious resource—my time—as I see fit. Everyone I know who has reached FI is doing more now in "retirement" than they were during their working years.

And this shouldn't surprise you! They have time, resources and the mental space to focus on what's important to them, how they can impact the world and who and what they want to spend time with and on. That's a marvelously liberating feeling and the pursuit of FI gives you the space to think about these deep and complex topics.

Brad's ideas about FI bring me back to the quote Tanja Hester of the blog *Our Next Life* shared with Brad and Jonathan: "We are some of the luckiest people in human history because we get to do the things we're excited about, that get us out of bed in the morning." That thought sends chills down my spine. It's such an amazing way to go through life.

FULLY FUNDED LIFESTYLE CHANGE

Once we reject the dichotomy of working or retirement, more interesting options to live a better life become apparent. One alternative to retirement is what Jay of *Slowly Sipping Coffee* called a "fully funded lifestyle change" (FFLC). He described this as having the freedom to live however you see fit. You can choose the path that creates the happiest and most satisfying life possible. This concept gives you the flexibility to pursue whatever option makes sense to you. This can mean becoming a stay-at-home parent, dropping from full-time to part-time work, choosing semi-retirement, taking a sabbatical or "mini-retirement," pursuing a lifestyle business, or combining these with other interesting ideas as they fit your life.

Jonathan latched on to this concept after talking to Jay on the podcast. At the same time he was talking to Jay and others in the FI community, Jonathan realized he couldn't keep the pace he was trying to maintain in his own life. He was working full-time as a pharmacist. His job was to keep people safe, requiring his full attention and effort. His job involved a significant daily commute. Meanwhile, he was putting in over forty hours per week on *ChooseFI* as it started to take off. Throw in a newborn son and life really got interesting.

Jonathan was constantly thinking about the next three or four things. Everything was urgent. He said, "I was just doing dumb stuff, like I would go fill up the car with gas and then I would leave the seal on the gas tank off because I had already moved onto the next mental object in my mind. And that's just a dangerous and stressful place to find yourself." He soon realized that something had to give.

Fall 2017 was an especially busy time for Jonathan, and he needed to take significant time off to explore opportunities that presented themselves related to *ChooseFI*. He had already planned a trip to visit his wife's family in Cape Town, South Africa. He decided to ask his boss for an unpaid leave of absence to give himself a few weeks to hit pause on the professional part of life. While he thought it was a reasonable request, his employer disagreed. His boss forced his hand by denying the request, informing Jonathan that he would have to step down to a lesser role if he wanted to take the time.

So he quit his job.

Jonathan said, "I don't think that was the answer he was expecting. I don't think you see that very often. But that is what happens when you get to a place in life where you're not just one to two months out from total financial disaster. You can make decisions that are in your best interest."

Jonathan's story had elements similar to Brad's story of using F-you money to leave his career as an accountant. But Jonathan was far from FI, or even half FI when he chose to cut the safety line. When digging out of debt, he cut expenses and simultaneously discovered that happiness didn't require spending a lot of money. Having no debt and minimal recurring expenses gave him the opportunity to make his decision from a position of strength. Power shifted from his employer to his side of the ledger. *Choose FI* became his life's project. The smart choices he made earlier in life enabled him to make the decision to pursue that project from a position of strength.

Having the financial freedom to live life on your own terms is the ultimate reason to *Choose FI*. Take a minute to reflect on the idea that you don't have to wait until you hit a magic number or a certain age to retire and experience that freedom. You begin to gain more freedom the day you *Choose FI*. That power continuously grows as you aggregate marginal gains while working toward the end goal of FI.

ACTION STEPS

1. **Vividly describe what your ideal day, week, and month would look like if money were not a concern.** Do you desire a traditional retirement with no work at age sixty or seventy? Would you like to retire sooner? Do you want to retire at all? If your current path is not taking you to your desired destination, determine what actions you need to take to start designing the life you want.

Never doubt that a small group of thoughtful, committed citizens can change the world; indeed, it's the only thing that ever has.

MARGARET MEAD

CONCLUSION

REDISCOVER POSSIBILITY

Throughout this book, I've tried to paint a picture of two very different paths through life. You can drift down the standard path, or you can *Choose FI*. Taking the less-worn path means you must make a conscious choice to change your mindset, followed by smaller sub-choices that enable you to choose your own adventures as you pursue a more rewarding life.

When you're stuck on the proverbial hamster wheel, it's hard to find time to stop running and take a breath. We get so bogged down keeping the wheel spinning that we rarely have time to think about anything else. When you *Choose FI*, you give yourself the chance to regain the wonder you had as a child, when anything was possible. No longer being beaten down by the world, you regain the ability to think big. As Jonathan frequently says, "You were born to do more than pay bills and die." That's easy to forget when you're stuck on the standard path. We tell our kids they can do and be anything they want, but how many adults actually live that out?

We live in a world that tells us life is hard. Politicians on the left and right tell us our lives will be better if we vote for them. Some think technology will save us. Our consumer culture sells the idea that happiness is a new car, a kitchen remodel, or a fancy vacation away. And there's always a way to pay. Just apply for a home equity loan or another credit card.

I hate to be the bearer of bad news, but no politician, technology, or consumer good is coming to fix what ails you. The superpower of FI starts with the choice to seek a better life and a belief that one is possible. But that choice and belief become real only when it is followed by action.

If there is a secret to *Choosing FI*, that's it. This book gives *you* the action steps to free yourself from the standard path. But freedom is only possible if you take the steps to empower yourself.

You can *Choose FI* and get off the hamster wheel. But what do you do with this freedom? What's the ultimate goal? Many start with the idea of achieving FIRE, but you can decouple FI and RE. FI makes work optional, without worrying about how you'll make your mortgage and car payments. You can stop paid work or choose to work because you enjoy it. When money is no longer the driving force behind your decisions, your motivations change.

Choosing FI is all about giving you the power to choose what you want. Many people envision retirement as a time of rest, relaxation, and recreation. There are certainly benefits to slowing down, focusing on relationships, and living a less stressful life. But if everyone who chooses FI opts for a life of leisure, our mission will have been a failure. FI is far bigger than retirement.

Once we are freed from the standard path and have the means to support ourselves indefinitely, we can shift our focus from day to day survival to thinking about bigger things. Carl of *1500*

Days to Freedom said, "I think we owe it to the world to give back in some way, either our time or money, at some point in life." Tanja Hester of *Our Next Life* shared a similar sentiment when asked what will determine if her efforts to achieve FI will have been worth it. She answered, "If we can ultimately leave the world a better place than we found it, if we can make a positive impact on people."

SPREADING THE SUPERPOWER

Making the decision to *Choose FI* will change your life. Achieving FI puts you in a position to be able to give freely of your time *and* money to change the lives of others. Being able to help change the world for the better, one person and one family at a time, is the ultimate driving force behind *Choose FI*.

When I originally reached out to Brad and Jonathan, I was attracted to the idea that they had already done a lot of what I originally considered the key legwork to make this project a success. They had already connected with many FI thought leaders, interviewed them, and collected key lessons. I thought finding those leaders and sharing their lessons was the *Choose FI* story. As this project has unfolded, I've realized there is a much bigger story. *Choose FI* isn't a top-down approach where a few gurus tell you how to do it. *Choose FI* is a community of like-minded people who want to connect and help one another improve their lives, working from the ground up.

The FI community is remarkable. Scott Rieckens, creator of the documentary *Playing With FIRE*, talked about this with Brad and Jonathan on the podcast. He said, "What I love the absolute most is I found an incredible community who actually seem to treat each other with respect, expand on ideas, challenge each other, and get to know each other, even in the comments sections of

blogs. I mean how many online communities can you say that about, where you actually see respect?"

It's not hard to understand this phenomenon. From a societal perspective, the FI community is marginalized. We're the weirdos because we use our money to build purposeful, meaningful, intentional lives in a society where "normal" is to spend every penny running from thing to thing in search of instant gratification.

Brad and Jonathan are making finding your tribe easier. They've formed local *ChooseFI* groups that allow people within local communities to organize and establish relationships with others in their immediate area. It's exciting to see these groups progress as they allow people to pool resources and ideas to live better lives and change their communities, one person and one family at a time.

Brad regularly talks about FI as a superpower. I understand this sentiment fully. *Choosing FI* has allowed me to experience things most of my peers could only imagine. I've traveled the world and had amazing experiences ranging from climbing 20,000-foot mountains to diving the Great Barrier Reef to attending Super Bowls. Not to mention I was able to walk away from my career at forty-one years old.

I now can choose to ski on powder days in the winter and take my daughter to the pool on hot sunny summer days. I'm not limited to going only on Saturdays, Sundays, or during my two weeks of vacation because those are the prescribed days off. I still work, but rather than following rules made by the boss and regulations created by bureaucrats, I choose the projects that I think are worthwhile and design meaningful work around my life instead of trying to fit my life around a work schedule.

Some people think they couldn't have this life because saving is too much of a sacrifice. The only things I've given up to achieve this lifestyle are paying interest to banks and credit card companies, excessive taxes to the government, and fees to my financial advisor.

Choosing FI is as simple as having the knowledge and motivation to do things a little bit smarter than those on the standard path through life. By taking action and accumulating small wins, you can create the life you want far faster than most believe is possible. Our goal is to share this message with as many people as possible so they understand that they too can *Choose FI*.

Brad, Jonathan, and I agree that spreading the message of *Choose FI* gives us an opportunity to change the world. As more people are shown the levers that can be pulled to achieve FI and are inspired by the stories of ordinary people who have unleashed these superpowers through their choices and actions, you see that you can free yourself from the chains that trap you on the standard path.

As we spread this message, I envision an army of smart, innovative, free-thinking people with the time and resources to tackle big problems. Is it overly ambitious to think that a small group of thoughtful, committed citizens can change the world? I agree with Margaret Mead: It's the only thing that ever has.

Get started today. Become a valuist. Commit to continued learning and growth. Start accumulating marginal gains. Stack your talents. Serve others by adding value to their lives. Invest wisely to create a perpetual money-making machine that will allow you to carve your own path through life without relying on a job.

Don't be afraid to be different. Your boss may question why you drive a ten-year-old car when you can afford the monthly payments for a new one. Your friends may call you cheap because you pack your lunch when you could afford to order takeout with them. Your family may ask why you wear socks with holes in them if you can afford to take a three-week international vacation.

Just be honest with them. Tell them you're making conscious choices because you're changing the world. Tell them you *Choose FI*.

ACTION STEPS

1. **Start Now.** Visit choosefi.com/start

2. **Do an 80/20 analysis of your life and finances.** This book provides the principles and tools to *Choose FI*. What single action can you take today to get started and have the greatest impact from the place you're starting?

3. **Revisit the chapters of this book that are most relevant as your situation changes.** Continue to learn, grow, and accumulate marginal gains as you create a reality that most only dream is possible.

4. **Join the closest local *ChooseFI* group and attend the next meet-up.** No group in your area yet? Start one and create your own group of FI peers and mentors to help you on your journey and who you will be able to help as you learn.

Put down the book and take action!

ACKNOWLEDGEMENTS

Thank you to my wife, Kim, for being my partner on the path to FI and all of my life's greatest adventures. I couldn't have done any of this without you.

Thank you Dad for spending countless hours on this project to help clarify my thoughts and turn my assault on the English language into a readable manuscript.

Thank you M.K. Williams for your ongoing feedback, support, and the countless behind the scenes, all too often thankless, tasks you've done to to get this project to the finish line.

Thank you Meghan Stevenson for your valuable feedback to shape and organize the content of this book and help us create a tone that makes the book inviting to anyone who wants to change their financial future.

Thank you Lorrie Grace Noggle for your immense efforts to help clarify our message in your role as copy editor.

Thank you Ellie Schroeder for bringing your amazing artistic talent and vision to this project to help bring the book to life, give it character, and make it unique.

Thank you Brad and Jonathan, for giving me a platform to share my story, allowing me unfettered access to your stories and material, and giving me the space and freedom to bring it together to create this resource to help and serve the next generation of the FI community. The FIRE is spreading!

Brad, Jonathan and I thank the members of the FI community who agreed to share their knowledge and experiences on the *ChooseFI* podcast and allow those interviews to be used as the basis of this book. *ChooseFI* is a crowd sourced platform that would not be possible without you.

BIBLIOGRAPHY

INTRODUCTION

Lund Fisker, Jacob. "Early Retirement Extreme." March 2019. http://earlyretirementextreme.com/

Lund Fisker, Jacob. "Day 3: Grocery Shopping." Early Retirement Extreme, December 12, 2008. http://earlyretirementextreme.com/day-3-grocery-shopping.html

Lund Fisker, Jacob. "Day 7: Going Car Free." Early Retirement Extreme, December 18, 2008. http://earlyretirementextreme.com/day-7-going-car-free.html

Berry Johnson, Janet. "What is the average APR on a credit card?" Credit Karma, January 2, 2019. https://www.creditkarma.com/credit-cards/i/average-apr-on-credit-card/

CHAPTER 1

Collins, JL. "Why you need F-you money." JLCollinsnh.com (blog), June 6, 2011. https://jlcollinsnh.com/2011/06/06/why-you-need-f-you-money/

U.S. Department of Commerce. *"Wealth, Asset Ownership, & Debt of Households Detailed Tables: 2011. "* Data. United States Census Bureau, 2011. https://www.census.gov/data/tables/2011/demo/wealth/wealth-asset-ownership.html

CHAPTER 2

Quartuccio, D. *Design Your Future: 3 Simple Steps to Stop Drifting and Take Command of Your Life*. (Create Space Independent Publishing, 2017).

Tim Ferriss, "Living Beautifully on $25-27K Per Year," February 13, 2017. The Tim Ferriss Show, podcast. https://tim.blog/2017/02/13/mr-money-mustache/

CHAPTER 3

Dweck, CS. *Mindset: The New Psychology of Success*. (New York: Penguin Random House, 2006.)

Adams S: *How to Fail at Almost Anything and Still Win Big: Kind of the Story of My Life*. (New York: Penguin Books, 2013.)

CHAPTER 4

Adeney, Pete, "The Shocking Simple Math Behind Early Retirement." Mr. Money Mustache Blog, January 13, 2012. https://www.mrmoneymustache.com/2012/01/13/the-shockingly-simple-math-behind-early-retirement/

Frankel, Matthew. "Here's the Average American's Savings Rate." The Motley Fool. October 3, 2016. https://www.fool.com/saving/2016/10/03/heres-the-average-americans-savings-rate.aspx

Pete Adeney, "Exposed! The MMM Family's 2016 Spending!" Mr. Money Mustache Blog, May 19, 2017. http://www.mrmoneymustache.com/2017/05/19/2016-spending/

Lund Fisker, Jacob. "Early Retirement Extreme."
http://earlyretirementextreme.com/

Saturday Night Live. Season 18, esisode 19, "Matt Foley: Van Down By The River." Aired May 8, 1993, on NBC. https://www. nbc.com/saturday-night-live/video/matt-foley-van-down-by-the-river/3505931.

CHAPTER 5

U.S. Department of Commerce. *"Wealth, Asset Ownership, & Debt of Households Detailed Tables: 2011. "* Data. United States Census Bureau, 2011. https://www.census.gov/data/tables/2011/demo/wealth/wealth-asset-ownership.html

Maynard, Micheline. "On Paying for Cars With Cash." *The New York Times*, July 28, 2007. https://www.nytimes.com/2007/07/28/business/yourmoney/28money.html

Edmunds. "Depreciation Infographic: How Fast Does My New Car Lose Value?" *Edmunds.com* (website), September 24, 2010. https://www.edmunds.com/car-buying/how-fast-does-my-new-car-lose-value-infographic.html

Bach, D. *The Automatic Millionaire: A Powerful One-Step Plan to Live and Finish Rich.* (New York: Crown Business, 2003.)

Blue Cross Blue Shield. "Blue Cross Blue Shield Health Index Identifies Top 10 Conditions Nationwide Affecting the Health of Commercially Insured." Blue Cross Blue Shield Association, March 1, 2018. https://www.bcbs.com/press-releases/blue-cross-blue-shield-health-index-identifies-top-10-conditions-nationwide

Wang, Jim "Here's the average net worth of American's at every age." Wallet Hacks (blog). *Business Insider* June 5, 2017. https://www.businessinsider.com/heres-the-average-net-worth-of-americans-at-every-age-2017-6

Wikipedia List of United States Mobile Virtual Network Operators: https://en.wikipedia.org/wiki/List_of_United_States_mobile_virtual_network_operators

CHAPTER 6

Ganch, Brandon. "Mad Fientist Archives." https://www.madfientist.com/archives/

Jacobson, Jeremy. "Never Pay Taxes Again." *Go Curry Cracker* (blog), October 26, 2013. https://www.gocurrycracker.com/never-pay-taxes-again/

McCurry, Justin. "$150,000 Income, $150 Income Tax." *Root of Good* (blog), October 16, 2013. https://rootofgood.com/make-six-figure-income-pay-no-tax/

United States Census Bureau. Income and Poverty in the United States: 2016." census.gov, September 12, 2017. https://www.census.gov/library/publications/2017/demo/p60-259.html

CHAPTER 7

N/A

CHAPTER 8

US Department of Education's Federal Student Aid Website: https://studentaid.ed.gov/sa/repay-loans/forgiveness-cancellation/public-service/questions

Carnevale, Anthony P., Cheah, Ban, and Hanson Andrew R, "The Economic Value of College Majors." Executive Summary. Georgetown University, Center on Education and the Workforce, McCourt School of Public Policy, 2015. https://cew.georgetown.edu/wp-content/uploads/Exec-Summary-web-B.pdf

Taylor, Paul, Fry, Rick and Oates, Russ, "The Rising Cost of Not Going to College." Pew Research Center Social and Demographic Trends. February 11, 2014. http://www.pewsocialtrends.org/2014/02/11/the-rising-cost-of-not-going-to-college/

United States Department of Labor. "Occupational Projections and Worker Characteristics. Bureau of Labor Statistics, 2016. https://www.bls.gov/emp/tables/occupational-projections-and-characteristics.htm#

CHAPTER 9

Ganch, Brandon. "The Power of Quitting." Mad Fientist (blog), August 2014. https://www.madfientist.com/power-of-quitting//

Ganch, Brandon. "The Time Has Finally Come." Mad Fientist (blog), March 2016. https://www.madfientist.com/time-has-finally-come/

CHAPTER 10

Miller, D. *48 Days to the Work You Love.* (Nashville, TN: B&H Books, 2007).

Harbinger, Jordan. "How to Rebuild a Business Using Your Network." March 22, 2018. *The Unstoppable CEO Podcast.* https://unstoppableceo.net/podcast/jordan-harbinger

Ferriss, Tim. *"General Stan McChrystal on Eating One Meal Per Day, Special Ops, and Mental Toughness."* The Tim Ferriss Show (podcast). March 6, 2015. https://tim.blog/2015/07/05/stanley-mcchrystal/

"Good Reads - Brian Tracy Quotes." https://www.goodreads.com/quotes/524183-invest-three-percent-of-your-income-in-yourself-self-development-in

CHAPTER 11

Adeney, Pete, "The Shocking Simple Math Behind Early Retirement." Mr. Money Mustache Blog, January 13, 2012. https://www.mrmoneymustache.com/2012/01/13/the-shockingly-simple-math-behind-early-retirement/

Collins J.L., *The Simple Path to Wealth.* (USA, Self-published, 2016).

CHAPTER 12

Merriman, Paul. "The Genius of John Bogle in 9 Quotes." *Marketwatch.* Nov. 25, 2016. https://www.marketwatch.com/story/the-genius-of-john-bogle-in-9-quotes-2016-11-23

Collins J.L., *The Simple Path to Wealth*. (USA, Self-published, 2016).

Collins, J.L. "How I Failed My Daughter and a Simple Path to Wealth" *JLCollinsnh.com* (blog), June 9, 2011. https://jlcollinsnh.com/2011/06/06/why-you-need-f-you-money/

Collins, J.L. "J.L. Collins Stock Series." https://jlcollinsnh.com/stock-series/

Bogle J. *The Little Book of Common Sense Investing*. (Hoboken, NJ: John Wiley and Sons, Inc., 2007).

Buffett, Warren. "Letter to the Shareholders of Berkshire Hathaway, Inc," February 28, 2014. http://www.berkshirehathaway.com/letters/2013ltr.pdf

"Bogleheads Lazy Portfolios". https://www.bogleheads.org/wiki/Lazy_portfolios

Merriman, Paul and Buck, Richard. "The Ultimate Buy and Hold Strategy: 2019 Update." *MarketWatch*, March 20, 2019. https://www.marketwatch.com/story/the-ultimate-buy-and-hold-strategy-2019-update-2019-03-20

CHAPTER 13

Kiyosaki, R. *Cash Flow Quadrants: Rich Dad's Guide to Financial Freedom*. (Scottsdale, AZ: Plata Publishing, 1998).

Ferriss, T. *The 4 Hour Work Week: Escape 9-5, Live Anywhere, and Join the New Rich*. (New York: Crown Publishing Group, 2007.)

CHAPTER 14

US Dept of Labor Bureau of Labor Statistics, *Issues in Labor Statistics*, March, 2002. https://www.bls.gov/opub/btn/archive/housing-expenditures.pdf

Carson, C. *Retire Early With Real Estate: How Smart Investing Can Help You Escape the 9-to-5 Grind and Do What Matters More.* (Denver, CO: Bigger Pockets Publishing, 2018).

Trench, S. *Set for Life: Planning Your Financial Future So You Can Live the Life You Choose.* (Denver, CO: Bigger Pockets Publishing, 2017).

CHAPTER 15

Adeney, Pete, "Mr. Money Mustache vs. the Internet Retirement Police" *Mr. Money Mustache Blog*, February 13, 2013. https://www.mrmoneymustache.com/2013/02/13/mr-money-mustache-vs-the-internet-retirement-police/

CONCLUSION

N/A

EPISODE REFERENCE

CHAPTER 1

Episode 18 with Jeremy of Go Curry Cracker:
https://www.choosefi.com/018-go-curry-cracker-capital-gains-losses-roth-conversion-ladder/

Episode 32 with Joel of FI 180:
https://www.choosefi.com/032-milestones-fi/

CHAPTER 2

Episode 14 with Carl of 1500 Days:
https://www.choosefi.com/014-phases-fi-mr-1500-days/

Episode 45 with J.D. Roth:
https://www.choosefi.com/045-jd-roth-get-rich-slowly/

Episode 12 with Liz from Frugalwoods:
https://www.choosefi.com/012-living-frugal/

Episode 27 with Jay of Slowly Sipping Coffee:
https://www.choosefi.com/027-slowly-sipping-coffee-fi-vs-risk-tolerance/

Episode 33 with Dominick Quartuccio:
https://www.choosefi.com/033-design-future/

Episode 24 with Joel and Alexis of Financial 180:
https://www.choosefi.com/024-fi180-make-u-turn-choose-fi/

Episode 40 with Becky and Noah of Money Metagame:
https://www.choosefi.com/040-take-gap-year-money-metagame/

Episode 37 with Scott Rieckens:
https://www.choosefi.com/037-playing-fire-documentary-scott-rieckens/

Episode 48 with the Happy Philosopher:
https://www.choosefi.com/048-happy-philosopher/

Episode 26 with Physician on FIRE:
https://www.choosefi.com/026-physician-on-fire/

Episode 52 with Todd Tresidder:
https://www.choosefi.com/052-todd-tresidder-risk-management/

Episode 15 with Justin of Root of Good:
https://www.choosefi.com/015-root-good-2nd-generation-fire-college/

Episode 39 with Gwen of Fiery Millennials:
https://www.choosefi.com/039-millennial-path-fi-fiery-millennial/

Episode 46 with Tanja Hester:
https://www.choosefi.com/046-ready-early-retirement-our-next-life-reveal/

CHAPTER 3

Episode 23 with ESI Money:
https://www.choosefi.com/023-career-hacking-esi-money/

Episode 49 with Alan Donegan and The Escape Artist:
https://www.choosefi.com/049-the-aggregation-of-marginal-gains/

CHAPTER 4

Episode 24 with Joel and Alexis of Financial 180:
https://www.choosefi.com/024-fi180-make-u-turn-choose-fi/

Episode 41 with Paige and Sam:
https://www.choosefi.com/041-high-cost-living-path-fi/

Episode 52 with Todd Tresidder:
https://www.choosefi.com/052-todd-tresidder-risk-management/

Episode 27 with Jay of Slowly Sipping Coffee:
https://www.choosefi.com/027-slowly-sipping-coffee-fi-vs-risk-tolerance/

Episode 12 with Liz from Frugalwoods:
https://www.choosefi.com/012-living-frugal/

Episode 48 with the Happy Philosopher:
https://www.choosefi.com/048-happy-philosopher/

Episode 14 with Carl of 1500 Days:
https://www.choosefi.com/014-phases-fi-mr-1500-days/

Episode 53 with Bobby Hoyt:
https://www.choosefi.com/053-millennial-money-man-do-you-want-to-be-rich/

CHAPTER 5

Episode 47 with Bryce and Kristi of Millennial Revolution:
https://www.choosefi.com/047-cult-of-home-ownership-millennial-revolution/

Episode 52 with Todd Tresidder:
https://www.choosefi.com/052-todd-tresidder-risk-management/

Episode 16 with Chad "Coach" Carson:
https://www.choosefi.com/016-house-hacking-coach-carson/

Episode 26 with Physician on FIRE:
https://www.choosefi.com/026-physician-on-fire/

Episode 41 with Paige and Sam:
https://www.choosefi.com/041-high-cost-living-path-fi/

Episode 12 with Liz from Frugalwoods:
https://www.choosefi.com/012-living-frugal/

Episode 27 with Jay of Slowly Sipping Coffee:
https://www.choosefi.com/027-slowly-sipping-coffee-fi-vs-risk-tolerance/

Episode 50 with Mr. Groovy:
https://www.choosefi.com/050-domestic-geoarbitrage-freedom-is-groovy/

Episode 48 with the Happy Philosopher: https://www.choosefi.com/048-happy-philosopher/

CHAPTER 6

Episode 17 with the Mad Fientist:
https://www.choosefi.com/017-mad-fientist-origin-story/

Episode 26 with Physician on FIRE:
https://www.choosefi.com/026-physician-on-fire/

Episode 40 with Becky and Noah of Money Metagame:
https://www.choosefi.com/040-take-gap-year-money-metagame/

Episode 18 with Jeremy of Go Curry Cracker:
https://www.choosefi.com/018-go-curry-cracker-capital-gains-losses-roth-conversion-ladder/

Episode 13 with Gerry Born:
https://www.choosefi.com/457b-free-money/

Episode 15 with Justin of Root of Good:
https://www.choosefi.com/015-root-good-2nd-generation-fire-college/

Episode 43 with Fitz Gilbert:
https://www.choosefi.com/043-drawdown-strategy-retirement-manifesto/

CHAPTER 7

Episode 17 with the Mad Fientist:
https://www.choosefi.com/017-mad-fientist-origin-story/

Episode 40 with Becky and Noah of Money Metagame:
https://www.choosefi.com/040-take-gap-year-money-metagame/

Episode 47 with Bryce and Kristi of Millennial Revolution:
https://www.choosefi.com/047-cult-of-home-ownership-millennial-revolution/

Episode 44 with Brandon Pearce:
https://www.choosefi.com/044-into-the-wind-brandon-pearce/

Episode 18 with Jeremy of Go Curry Cracker:
https://www.choosefi.com/018-go-curry-cracker-capital-gains-losses-roth-conversion-ladder/

Episode 37 with Scott Rieckens:
https://www.choosefi.com/037-playing-fire-documentary-scott-rieckens/

Episode 50 with Mr. Groovy:
https://www.choosefi.com/050-domestic-geoarbitrage-freedom-is-groovy/

Episode 26 with Physician on FIRE:
https://www.choosefi.com/026-physician-on-fire/

CHAPTER 8

Episode 78 with Travis Hornsby:
https://www.choosefi.com/078-student-loan-debt-repayment-travis-hornsby/

Episode 87 with Don Wettrick:
https://www.choosefi.com/087-education-through-innovation-don-wettrick/

Episode 49 with Alan Donegan and The Escape Artist:
https://www.choosefi.com/049-the-aggregation-of-marginal-gains/

Episode 89 with Robert Farrington:
https://www.choosefi.com/089-retail-path-to-fi-with-college-investor/

Episode 83 with Cody Berman:
https://www.choosefi.com/083-second-generation-fi-cody-berman/

Episode 40 with Becky and Noah of Money Metagame:
https://www.choosefi.com/040-take-gap-year-money-metagame/

Episode 39 with Gwen of Fiery Millennials:
https://www.choosefi.com/039-millennial-path-fi-fiery-millennial/

Episode 16 with Chad "Coach" Carson:
https://www.choosefi.com/016-house-hacking-coach-carson/

CHAPTER 9

Episode 16 with Chad "Coach" Carson:
https://www.choosefi.com/016-house-hacking-coach-carson/

Episode 23 with ESI Money:
https://www.choosefi.com/023-career-hacking-esi-money/

CHAPTER 10

Episode 47 with Bryce and Kristi of Millennial Revolution:
https://www.choosefi.com/047-cult-of-home-ownership-millennial-revolution/

Episode 63 with Scott Trench:
https://www.choosefi.com/063-scott-trench-set-life/

CHAPTER 11

N/A

CHAPTER 12

Episode 19 with JL Collins:
https://www.choosefi.com/019-jlcollinsnh-stock-series-part-1/

Episode 34 with JL Collins:
https://www.choosefi.com/034-stock-series-part-2-jl-collins/

Episode 36 with JL Collins:
https://www.choosefi.com/036-community-chatauqua-ama-jl-collins/

Episode 35 with Big ERN:
https://www.choosefi.com/035-sequence-return-risk-early-retirement-now/

CHAPTER 13

Episode 52 with Todd Tresidder
https://www.choosefi.com/052-todd-tresidder-risk-management/

Episode 30 with Alan Donegan:
https://www.choosefi.com/030-side-hustle-unspoken-lever-fi/

Episode 53 with Bobby Hoyt:
https://www.choosefi.com/053-millennial-money-man-do-you-want-to-be-rich/

Episode 44 with Brandon Pearce:
https://www.choosefi.com/044-into-the-wind-brandon-pearce/

Episode 49 with Alan Donegan and The Escape Artist:
https://www.choosefi.com/049-the-aggregation-of-marginal-gains/

CHAPTER 14

Episode 16 with Chad "Coach" Carson:
https://www.choosefi.com/016-house-hacking-coach-carson/

Episode 63 with Scott Trench:
https://www.choosefi.com/063-scott-trench-set-life/

Episode 52 with Todd Tresidder:
https://www.choosefi.com/052-todd-tresidder-risk-management/

Episode 52R with contribution from Big ERN:
https://www.choosefi.com/052r-bring-just-getting-started/

CHAPTER 15

Episode 48 with the Happy Philosopher:
https://www.choosefi.com/048-happy-philosopher/

Episode 17 with the Mad Fientist:
https://www.choosefi.com/017-mad-fientist-origin-story/

Episode 52 with Todd Tresidder:
https://www.choosefi.com/052-todd-tresidder-risk-management/

Episode 45 with J.D. Roth:
https://www.choosefi.com/045-jd-roth-get-rich-slowly/

Episode 43 with Fitz Gilbert:
https://www.choosefi.com/043-drawdown-strategy-retirement-manifesto/

Episode 46 with Tanja Hester:
https://www.choosefi.com/046-ready-early-retirement-our-next-life-reveal/

Episode 27 with Jay of Slowly Sipping Coffee:
https://www.choosefi.com/027-slowly-sipping-coffee-fi-vs-risk-tolerance/

CONCLUSION

Episode 14 with Carl of 1500 Days:
https://www.choosefi.com/014-phases-fi-mr-1500-days/

Episode 46 with Tanja Hester:
https://www.choosefi.com/046-ready-early-retirement-our-next-life-reveal/

Episode 37 with Scott Rieckens:
https://www.choosefi.com/037-playing-fire-documentary-scott-rieckens/

ABOUT THE AUTHORS

CHRIS MAMULA

Chris regularly writes about financial independence while expanding the conversation around what retirement is and can be found at CanIRetireYet.com. His articles have been featured on MarketWatch, DoughRoller, and Business Insider. He achieved financial independence and retired from his physical therapy career in 2017, at the age of 41. In addition to writing, he now focuses on being a dedicated husband, stay at home dad and dirtbag/ski-bum depending on the season at his home in the mountains of Utah.

BRAD BARRETT

After years in public accounting as a CPA, Brad reached financial independence at the age of 35 through diligent savings and investing. Brad Is passionate about everything from saving money, to living a life focused on health, fitness, relationships and an empowering mindset, to 'boring' things like tracking your finances and cutting down on your tax bill. But his favorite topic is leveraging credit card rewards to save more money, and take trips you never would have dreamed possible for pennies on the dollar.

JONATHAN MENDONSA

Prior to discovering the financial independence / early retirement movement, Jonathan Mendonsa followed the "normal path," which ultimately led him to graduate pharmacy school at the age of 28 with $168,000 in student loans. Now, four years later, he has clawed his way out of debt and is aggressively pursuing financial independence. From his own experience, Jonathan is passionate about the pursuit of financial independence and its power to change lives. He is thrilled to share his experiments in life optimization as a co-host of the *ChooseFI* podcast.

Brad and Jonathan have been featured by Time, Forbes, BBC, The Wall Street Journal and Kiplinger. In the words of Jean Chatzky, The Today Show's Financial Editor, "it (the FI movement) has grown to be a movement in large part because of a podcast called *ChooseFI*.

CPSIA information can be obtained
at www.ICGtesting.com
Printed in the USA
BVHW031005160720
583883BV00002B/222

9 780960 058907